God: A Self Portrait

Maris,

Thank you for your ministry

Phillip Michael

God: A Self Portrait

Philip McCarty

iUniverse, Inc.
New York Lincoln Shanghai

God: A Self Portrait

iUniverse, Inc.

For information address:
iUniverse, Inc.
2021 Pine Lake Road, Suite 100
Lincoln, NE 68512
www.iuniverse.com

ISBN: 0-595-33463-6

Printed in the United States of America

Contents

THE FINAL TOUCHES: THE COMBINATION CHARACTERISTICS

Welcome

Curious about God? If you answered yes to this question, then you are a seeker, and I welcome you to this look at who God is and what He is like.

There are some people who are still trying to find God. Then, there are those who have found Him and are still seeking a deeper relationship with Him. The first is a new seeker, the other a veteran. But, both are seekers.

For thirty-four years I have followed God. And yet, I still seek a deeper relationship with Him. It is my desire to know God better every day. You might think that is impossible after a person grows up in church, graduates from a Bible college, and becomes an ordained minister. But, if doing this project has shown me anything, it is that God is so deep, I will always find something new to amaze me.

This book is for seekers. It is intended for those who are at the beginning of their exploration of God. If you have never been to church, or maybe you just started, I hope this book will benefit you. With this in mind I have tried very hard not to allow myself to use "church speak" or "Christianese" language without properly defining it first. There is no reason for the language to not be clear, even though we will be tackling some difficult concepts.

But, while the language is understandable, and the intended reader is new to the whole idea of God, this is still a book that can touch the veteran seeker. There is nothing new here. I will not be presenting any new truths about God. But, hopefully, the truth has been presented in a fresh way that will cause even the veteran seeker to see God in a new light.

We are not going to waste time by trying to prove the existence of God. From its very first words, "In the beginning God," the Bible assumes the existence of this Deity, and so will we. Besides, other authors, much more learned than I, have taken on this task, and their books are available.

This is not to say that if you do not believe in God that you need to throw this book down and run to another. The fact that you picked up this book shows that there is something within you that wants to seek the truth about God. You are on the front end of your exploration. I encourage you to read this study. Think about it. Mull it over and chew on it for a while. Let this be the beginning of your search. After all, you have to start somewhere, why not here?

The title of this study is a little different: <u>God: A Self Portrait</u>. What does that mean? It means that I believe there is a God, and that He is far beyond our capability to see or understand. The only way we could ever know that God existed would be for Him to reveal Himself to us. The only way we could understand His characteristics would be for Him to show us. God would have to create a self portrait because man could never paint an accurate picture of the unimaginable God with watercolors or words.

God chose to reveal Himself, to paint His portrait, in two ways. First, there is general revelation, better known as creation. What He has created; this universe, this earth, each and every person; is a reflection of some characteristic of God. We see His intelligence and orderliness. We see His attention to detail and His love for beauty. His imagination and power are evident everywhere. Each and every creation can teach us something about its Creator, but none more so than God's greatest creation, humans.

The portrait has also developed through God's giving us specific revelation, written words to describe Himself and His ways. We call this the Bible. No other book gives us such an accurate picture of God. For this particular study we are going to focus our attention on what the Bible has to say about God instead of trying to beg glimpses from creation. The Bible is believed to be God's word to man. As such, it is our greatest reference for fleshing out this portrait God has given to us. What kind of a portrait of God do we find in the Bible? Is He the kindly old man on a throne granting wishes, or the cosmic killjoy making rules to keep us from having fun, and zapping us with lightning bolts? We will see.

This study divides God's characteristics, or attributes, into three sections. The first section will look at the physical characteristics of God. What does God look like physically? How old is God? How big is God? These are some of the questions we will try to answer as we look into God's physical characteristics.

The next section deals with God's moral characteristics. We have all probably heard that God is good, but what makes Him that way? What are the moral absolutes in God's character? Are they just ideas He holds to, or are they part of His actual being? We will try to answer those questions.

The final section deals with characteristics of God that I believe involve the combination of both the physical and moral attributes. Included in these characteristics are God's right to rule, and His wisdom. We will also discuss the fact that all of the physical and moral characteristics of God are absolute and cannot change.

As we go through this study, it will be important for you to read the scripture references given in the text. If you are like most people today, you might be a little stumped when it comes to trying to find things in the Bible. Let me give you some hints that might help. First, like most other books, the Bible has a Table of Contents. Use it as much as you need to help you find the books of the Bible. Some people call it the most important page in the Bible.

Second, allow me to show you how to read a reference to scripture such as, Exodus 20:3. The Bible is divided into books, with most of the books having chapters, and all having verses. Exodus is the book of the Bible. The number in front of the colon is the chapter of that book, and the numbers after the colon are the verse or verses to be read.

Finally, it is a good idea to find a Bible that you can understand when you read it. There are many translations out there for you to choose from. Usually a Christian bookstore is more than happy to help you find one that fits you. I have purposely just used references to texts instead of quotes from a particular translation. That way you can read the words for yourself, and get used to your own Bible.

The Bible tells us in Genesis that man was created in God's image. As such, the more we know what God is like, the more we will understand what we are to be like. So, as we go through this study we will also be developing our own self portrait. Each characteristic of God will be related to us in a section I will call "Brush Strokes." Here we will see how the perfections of God are to be fleshed out in imperfect humans. Hopefully we will be able to come to a better understanding of ourselves, as we see the awesome portrait of God revealed before our eyes.

This is not an all inclusive look at the portrait of God. At best, it is little more than a child's crayon drawing. But, this study has broadened my understanding of God and myself. My hope is that it will do the same for you. So, once again, welcome. Enter into this gallery displaying the self portrait God has given us.

DRAWING THE LINES

THE PHYSICAL CHARACTERISTICS OF GOD

◆

SPIRIT
TRINITY
ETERNAL/SELF-EXISTENT
EVERYWHERE PRESENT/
IMMENSE
KNOWS EVERYTHING
ALMIGHTY

God Is Spirit

It must be completely understood as we begin our study that God is not like us. Over the centuries people have come to picture God as this wise old man with special powers who sits on a throne in heaven. They see God as a kindly grandfather granting wishes, and then are disappointed when things do not go the way they expected. But, God is not a man. He does not look like a man.

John 4:24 clearly states that "God is a Spirit." What does this mean? When we think of the word spirit, we often get a picture of a ghost in our mind. We see a human form that is disembodied, floating through the air, and transparent. Is this really what God is? Let's study this out and see how God has described Himself in His word.

God Is Above His Creation

We find the Ten Commandments in the book of Exodus, chapter 20. These are the famous commandments given to Moses by God on the tablets of stone at Mount Sinai. The commandments tell us how we are to relate to God and to each other.

The second commandment is found in verses 4-6 of that chapter. God commands that we not make any kind of image of anything that has been created in order to bow down to worship it. This means that worship of the stars and the sun and moon are out. Worship of trees and animals is out. Worship of any fish, or the ocean, is out. Worshipping man is not allowed, and neither is worshipping the earth. We are not to worship anything that God created, and we are not to make any kind of representation and say that this is what God looks like.

In verse 5, God declares that He is a jealous God, and will not put up with such actions. God understood that such false worship would be passed down from generation to generation. He declares that He will never allow it. Even after several generations of this false worship, God would still be against it. He will never say, "OK, if that's the way you want to think about Me, then I will go along with it." God is 100% against us making representations of Him. It makes Him angry and vengeful, and He will never compromise on this point.

But, God goes on in verse 6 to declare that those who worship Him the way He has prescribed will be blessed. They will be shown love and mercy. This means that if the father worshipped a fish as God, but the son realized the truth and started worshipping God in the way he was supposed to, God would show mercy to the son, and love him.

Moses repeats this commandment in Deuteronomy 4:15-24. This is one of Moses' farewell speeches to the people of Israel, who he had been leading for 40 years. He prefaces the repeating of this commandment by reminding the people how they got the commandments in the first place.

The people were at the mountain, and what looked like fire appeared on the mountain. Moses went up and God gave him the commandments to give to the people. Moses points out in his speech that the people did not see any kind of a shape, or form, to this manifestation of God. It was just a shapeless glowing mass, like fire. So, he reminds the people of the second commandment to not make an image and say that "this is what God looks like."

Moses goes on to give a list of specific creatures or objects that were not to be used to represent God. Unfortunately, throughout the centuries all of these have been used by people in worship. Several cultures have had gods and goddesses that looked like men and women. Among these were the Egyptian, Roman, and Greek religions. Neither the male, nor the female was to be worshipped, or held up as a representation of God. Animals were worshipped in past civilizations, and even today some of the tribal cultures still worship animal deities. Some cultures even created mutations of animals and man and worshipped them. Astrology is still prominent today as people check their horoscopes believing that the stars are what control the universe instead of God.

Once again, Moses reiterates the fact that God is a jealous God. He will not tolerate us worshipping something He has created instead of worshipping Him.

God poses a question in Isaiah 40:25 and 26. He wants to know what part of creation is equal to the Creator? Obviously the Creator is above His creation. So, how could we possibly take something from that creation and make it represent God? It would be like a computer taking a hard drive and saying, "This is what my creator looks like." God is far above His creation. Nothing is equal to Him in power, intelligence, or form.

So, why is God such a stickler about this point? Why is it so important that we not represent God in some way by making a shape to represent Him? Because, when we represent God with an object, we make Him equal with that object. God is adamant that His true being not be cheapened or reduced by portraying it as one of His creations. God is unique, distinct, and unable to be reproduced.

God Is Beyond His Creation

The Bible teaches that God is beyond the physical perception of that which He created. Jesus says that "No one has seen God" (John 1:18). Later on Jesus states that "No one has seen or heard God" (John 5:37). The true being of God has never been seen by the human eye. The true voice of God has never been heard by the human ear.

In his writings, the Apostle Paul calls God invisible (1 Timothy 1:17 and Colossians 1:15). Paul was saying that God cannot be seen by human eyes. He is invisible to us, yet His presence is still there.

Remember that God is a Spirit. He is not like us. When Jesus was resurrected from the dead, He presented Himself to the disciples in the upper room. He actually walked through the wall, or the closed door, of a locked room. The disciples were scared when He did this. I can't say I blame them. But Jesus calmed them down by telling them to touch Him. He wanted them to see that He did have flesh and bones. He was not a spirit, or ghost. The implication is that a spirit is not bound by flesh. It is a different substance than the physical bodies we find here on earth. Without flesh a spirit is free and limitless.

God is a free and limitless being. We can never see His true being because he is beyond our realm of comprehension. This point has to be understood, or else the rest of this study will be confusing. God is not bound by anything. As we go through this study we will see that this is true.

Allow me one more, important quote from God, which is definitive on this matter of God being beyond His creation. It also leads into the next point we need to look at concerning God being a Spirit.

The story is related in Exodus 33:18-23. Moses has spoken with God, and received the Ten Commandments, among other instructions for the people of Israel. Of all the people who have lived since Adam and Eve, Moses has had the closest relationship with God. And yet, in this encounter, Moses is asking God to reveal His face. Moses wants to see the true being of God in all His glory. "No one can see me and live," God replies (v.20). Any human who actually saw the true being of God would not survive. It would be too much. God is definitely beyond His creation.

God Is Revealed To His Creation

Let us stay with the Exodus 33 account as we begin to look at how God reveals Himself to His creation, specifically humans. It is obvious that something has appeared to represent God's being at various times, including this point in Exodus. Abraham saw God in human form and spoke with Him about Sodom and Gomorrha (The Angel of God in Genesis 18 and 19). Moses had already seen God in the form of a pillar of fire and a pillar of a cloud when He led them out of Egypt (Exodus 13:21 and 14:19). Moses also had seen the fire on Mount Sinai when he received the commandments. Later, Moses would see the presence of God enter the tabernacle as a fire and cloud (Exodus 40:34-38). So, if no one can see God, then what is it that Moses and others are seeing?

What Moses and others saw were physical manifestations God used to reveal His presence to the people. God allowed His presence to be made known through forms that we could see and understand. Fire, clouds, dove, and even a human form are just some of the ways God made His presence known. It seems that God may have taken human form in Exodus 34:5 in order to talk with Moses face to face. But all of these manifestations are not the true being of God, they are just forms or images God creates to display His presence. So, the true being of God has never been seen by anyone, only the manifestations of His presence which God chose to use. It is the true being of God that Moses asked to see in Exodus 33.

Because we cannot see or understand the true nature of God, we have to use anthropomorphic expressions. In other words, we have to assign human characteristics, to God's being, or sometimes animal characteristics such as wings. Even God uses human characteristics to describe Himself to Moses in Exodus 33. God talks about Moses not being able to see His face, and that He would cover him with His hand. Moses would only be allowed to see the back of God. Face, hand and back are all anthropomorphic expressions to help Moses understand and grasp the concept God was trying to share with him. God was telling Moses that he could not view the full being of God (His face). In order to keep Moses from seeing something that would kill him, God was going to protect him (cover him with his hand). Moses would be allowed to see only a portion of God which God would reveal (His back).

While God does make His presence known through various physical manifestations, creation never sees the full being of God. As such, in order to talk about God and try to have a frame of reference for grasping and understanding Him, we must use anthropomorphic expressions. We have to assign physical characteristics to God. If we did not use anthropomorphic expressions, or describe God in terms we could understand, we would have no way of relating to God, or understanding anything about Him. But our vocabulary can never describe the incomprehensible.

With all of this in mind, we need to ask another question. Why do we see God as being male? We always refer to God as being He, and Jesus referred to Him as Father. But, God is a Spirit, and is neither male nor female.

Gender is a trait given to the created beings of animals and humans. God made humans male and female. Neither can survive without the other. A species of all males, or all females, would die out.

Man was given the responsibility to care for his family, to provide for them and lead them. With that great responsibility comes great accountability. The man is to be the leader of his home, but not a dictator. He is to protect his family from harm, and make decisions that will promote the safety and welfare of his wife and children.

This responsibility reaches beyond the confines of a man's family. It stretches into the far regions of his community. He is to protect others from harm, and make decisions which benefit the safety and welfare of others. He is to stand for those who cannot stand for themselves. The protection and welfare of the whole society is in the hands of those men who are living up to their responsibility.

The woman was given a special bond with her children in order to teach them and raise them to be significant contributors to the world. She was designed by God with an incredible instinct and propensity for protecting her children at all costs. If you doubt this special bond, then just remember that the sports players almost always turn to the camera and say "Hi Mom", not "Hi Dad."

Like men, women's responsibility goes beyond the family and into the community. She is to influence and guide the next generation in the principles that will make them strong contributors to their society. She is to work to protect the next generation, in whatever way she can. Society's greatest asset is its children. Each generation needs strong women fulfilling their responsibility to see that the next generation will be great.

When we view God, when we think of His character, we see Him as being responsible for our welfare. He is to provide for us and take care of us. He is to make decisions that are for our best interest, and to protect us. Therefore, we consider God to have the same responsibilities as man, only on a universal order. That is why God is usually referred to as He. That is why Jesus referred to Him as Father. God has the same responsibility as He gave man.

But, God also has a side where He is a teacher, and has a strong bond with His creation. In that sense, God has a feminine side. God is neither male nor female. He is Spirit. But, when He created humans, he appears to have given males one part of His characteristics, and females the other part. It is only by working together that we get a better picture of the true nature of God. So, it appears that

God has revealed a part of himself, even in the responsibilities He has given to men and women.

Conclusion

God is a Spirit. The Bible teaches that God is above His creation. He is far greater than anything ever created, and therefore should not be lowered by making Him equal to something that was created. God is beyond His creation. We cannot understand, or even see, His true being. As a Spirit, God is without limitations. The physical rules that apply in creation do not apply to Him. God has revealed Himself to His creation through physical manifestations which we are able to understand. He has even revealed part of His character by the responsibilities He gave to both men and women.

So, what is a Spirit? It is beyond description, beyond physical limitations or form. This is the base of our study. If we cannot grasp the fact that God is unlike anything we know, then we will never understand the remainder of this study. He is so far above us, yet He still finds ways to make Himself known.

Brush Strokes

What about us? How does God being Spirit have any application in our life?

Remember that when God created male and female, He gave them each a set of responsibilities. Each of these responsibilities reflected characteristics of God. If both male and female have responsibilities which are characteristics of God, then how can we ever say that one gender is more important than another? Both are representative of God and we should never demean that representation. To do so is to demean God, to lower His value in that responsibility.

Each person must fulfill their God given responsibility according to the situation in which they find themselves. Some people are single, others married. Some have children, others do not. Whatever our situation, we must strive to carry out our responsibility, whether it is in family or community. As we carry out the responsibilities given to our gender by God, we become a picture of the character of God. The handling of this responsibility becomes a brush stroke within our own character as we make visible a portion of the unseen Spirit called God.

- *While God is neither male nor female, I will still use the masculine pronoun for God because it is common usage, and it speaks of His great responsibility toward us.*

The Trinity Declared

In the last chapter we discovered that God is a Spirit, He is far beyond anything we have ever seen or experienced in this world. His physical form, and the true substance of His being, is outside our ability to comprehend. Along those same lines we are now going to look at another aspect of God which has confused even the most intelligent of theologians over the ages. The doctrine of the trinity will once again show us that God is not anything like us physically.

The word "trinity" does not appear in the Bible. In other words, the Bible never states emphatically that "God is a trinity" like it states "God is a Spirit." But this does not mean that this is not true about God. The real problem with this characteristic of God is that we cannot adequately define it. Spirit was hard enough to define, but the trinity is a concept that our human vocabulary just cannot express. Over the years many intelligent people have tried to define this aspect of God, and the closest they have come is the word trinity.

So, what is the trinity? Within the Bible we find that God is defined as one God, a single entity or being. But, we also find that there are three "beings" who are designated as God; the Father, the Son, and the Holy Spirit. The idea of the trinity is that we have three that are one, and one which is three. One of the problems is identifying the different components. We do not know exactly what to call them. They are not three separate beings because they all three act as one. They are not just personalities because they have a physical form. We are left with a mystery that is God; three individual characters, yet one being.

In this chapter we will look at how the Bible relates the portrait of the trinity. While we may never understand it or comprehend it, hopefully we will be able to at least grasp the concept that God is more than just a simple being.

The Bible Declares There Is One God

The very first of the Ten Commandments (Exodus 20:3) tells us that God is the only God in the universe. There are no other gods who are to be worshipped, because there are no other true gods. No other gods are above Him in any way.

For the Jews coming out of Egypt where there was a god for everything, this would be a new concept. Only one God is true and to be worshipped.

Moses reiterates this thought of there only being one God in Deuteronomy 4:35 and 39. There is no one else beside, or above, or instead of God. The call to worship for Israel was given to them later in that same book (Deuteronomy 6:4). It says, "Hear O Israel: The Lord our God is one Lord." The unity and oneness of God is stressed even in the early days of God's relationship with the people of Israel.

Several times in the book of Isaiah God declares that He is the only God, specifically chapter 45, verses 18, 21 and 22. God is trying to show Israel that there are no other gods besides Him. He is the only true God. The idols they were worshipping were false, meaningless blocks of wood and stone and metal. God is the only true living God. In Isaiah 46:9, God states this truth twice for emphasis.

Let's not think that the New Testament writers abandoned the one God for several Gods. Paul, in his first letter to the Corinthians, tells them that there is no such thing as other Gods, but only lifeless idols. He states clearly the belief that there is only one God (1 Corinthians 8:4-6). However, Paul goes on to place Jesus as an equal to God. But how could God the Father and Jesus be equal? How could two beings be considered God and yet God be just one being? Paul does not elaborate or try to explain this. He simply accepts it as a truth and moves on.

The early church as a whole believed that there was only one God. Paul tries to encourage the church in Ephesus to keep living the Christian life in unity by quoting to them parts of an early church creed (Ephesians 4:4-6). This creed stresses the oneness found in the Christian relationship with God and each other. Verse 6 tells us that they believed in only one God, not multiple Gods.

The book of James also talks about the importance of knowing there is only one God. James 2:19 shows the importance of having this belief as a base for your understanding of God, but at the same time not letting it be the only thing you believe.

So, we can see that God has revealed Himself as a single entity, or being. He is adamant that there are no other beings who are to be considered God. This is shown by the very first commandment He gave to Moses, and His insistence throughout the Old Testament that He is the one and only God. And we have found that the New Testament does not contradict this picture of God. Paul and the early church believed that there was only one God.

The Bible Declares Three Beings as God

God the Father

In the Old Testament, God portrays Himself as a father (Isaiah 63:16; 64:8; Jeremiah 3:4,19; 31:9; Malachi 1:6). This is the standard picture of God seen throughout the Old Testament. He is constantly referring to Israel as His children, which reinforces this picture.

When Jesus comes along in the New Testament, He refers to God as His Father. The Apostles and writers of the New Testament held to God being Father (Romans 8:15; 2 Corinthians 1:3; Ephesians 4:6).

God the Son

The Old Testament suggests that there is another part of God which had not yet been revealed to them. Isaiah 9:6-7 tells us that there will be a future king of Israel who will be called "Mighty God, Everlasting Father." No mere man could hold those titles without breaking the first commandment, and possibly even the second. The only way someone could legitimately be given those titles without breaking the commandments is to be God. This means that God would take on human flesh and walk the earth.

In Matthew 22:41-46, we see Jesus verbally sparring with the religious leaders. He had just passed a series of tests these leaders had given Him, trying to trip Him up so they could arrest Him. Now, Jesus gives them a test. He refers to Psalm 110:1, and asks them how David, who was the highest King of Israel, could ever call one of his sons "Lord"? David would always be king over anyone who came after him, and therefore would not submit to them by calling them Lord. Yet, David, in his Psalm, calls one of his heirs Lord. Who could this heir be that would be greater than David? The answer, of course, is God. God would be a descendant of David in human flesh.

So, we see that there are statements in the Old Testament that show that God was going to take on human flesh, even though they were not completely understood until Jesus came. Jesus declared that He was God walking on earth.

Another confrontation between Jesus and the religious leaders is recorded in John 8:21-59. Jesus, in the early part of this argument, declares that He comes from above, which means heaven (23). He is already saying He is not of this world; He is someone who is supernatural. The argument degenerates into a question of lineage. These people were descendants of Abraham and they felt they had a special relationship with God because of that.

Jesus tells the religious leaders that Abraham was glad to see His day. They do not understand this. They think Jesus is crazy. At this time Jesus is only a little over thirty years old and Abraham had died hundreds of years before. How could Abraham have seen Jesus, or Jesus been with Abraham?

The climax to this confrontation comes with Jesus' answer in verse 58, "Before Abraham was, I Am." When Moses asked God what His name was so he could tell the people which God sent him to free them from Egypt, God said, "Tell them I Am has sent you" (Exodus 3:13-14). I Am was the sacred name of God, and Jesus used it to refer to Himself. The religious leaders understood this and picked up stones to kill Jesus. Anyone making himself out to be God should be put to death according to their law. It broke the first commandment.

God declared Jesus to be His Son at Jesus' baptism (Matthew 3:16-17). At the transfiguration of Jesus, God also declared Jesus to be His Son (Matthew 17:5).

Thomas, one of Jesus' disciples, declares Jesus to be God in a face-to-face encounter after the resurrection (John 20:28). On the Day of Pentecost, Peter delivers a sermon in which he uses some of the same arguments Jesus did, to declare that Jesus is God (Acts 2). Paul preached Jesus to those in Athens, declaring Him to be their unknown God, the true God (Acts 17:22-31). Paul opens his letter to the Romans by declaring Jesus as God (Romans 1:1-7). Throughout the New Testament we see Jesus being declared as God.

The Holy Spirit

From the opening words of the Bible, we see the Spirit of God mentioned. Genesis 1:2 says that the Spirit of God was involved in creation. As we move through the Old Testament we see the Spirit of God being considered the same as God the Father. The writers did not make a distinction between the two entities.

As God led the people of Israel out of Egypt, He gave Moses instructions for how to build a tabernacle in which to put the Ark of the Covenant. This tent complex was to have several different courts, places which were covered for only the priests to enter, and one place where only the high priest could enter once a year. It was also to have golden candlesticks, altars, a basin for ceremonial washing, and other things related to the worship of God. In order to build all this to the specifications God gave, and to make sure the work was quality work, the Spirit of God filled a particular craftsman to oversee and do the work (Exodus 31:1-5).

The book of Judges has the people of Israel finally in the land that they were promised. They have conquered most of the land, but still have enemies. Throughout the book we are told that the Spirit of God comes upon certain men and gives them strength and wisdom in leading Israel in battle against their enemies.

The most famous of these judges, as they were called, is Samson. Yes, the one with the long hair. Samson was often filled with the Spirit of God and given great strength (Judges 13:25; 14:6,19; 15:14). His long hair was a symbol of his dependence on God. When he gave up his secret to his girl friend and his hair was cut, Samson was showing that he had begun to rely on himself instead of God. The spirit of God only entered him one more time after that, just long enough to bring down the building he was in, killing many of the enemy along with himself (Judges 16:28-30).

The book of 1 Samuel tells us that the first king of Israel, Saul, was filled with the Spirit of God (10:5-10). It also relates that the second, and most prominent, king, David, was filled with the Spirit of God (16:13). Throughout the rest of the Old Testament the Spirit of God is mentioned.

In His last discussion with the disciples before His death, Jesus tells them that God will send a Comforter to them when He is gone (John 14:16). He calls this Comforter the Spirit of Truth (v.17). Later on He identifies this Comforter as the Holy Ghost (v.26). The terms Holy Ghost and Holy Spirit are synonymous in the New Testament.

Peter led off his sermon in Acts 2 with a reference to the Holy Spirit as God (vs. 15-18). He is quoting from the book of Joel, an Old Testament prophet who said that in the last days God would pour out His Spirit on men. This is a definite statement by Peter that the Holy Spirit is God. God was now dwelling within men. This belief was held at the very beginning of the church, it was not thought up later to try to confuse people.

Acts 5:1-11 relates an incident in the early church. Two people, husband and wife, sold some land and promised to give all of the proceeds to God. They lied about the price they received for the land and kept some of the money for themselves. Now, keeping the money was not wrong. But, it was wrong to say that they had given all of the money to the church when they really had not. They were trying to make themselves look better to others instead of truly worshipping God with a gift.

Peter calls these people on their lie. He tells them they have lied to God (Acts 5:4). Then in Acts 5:9 he tells them they have conspired to tempt the Spirit of the Lord. The idea here is that the Spirit of the Lord is equated with God.

The first martyr of the church is found in Acts 7. Stephen was a deacon, a leader who helps in the church. Just as the people are getting ready to stone him, Stephen gives his last sermon. Within it he relates the history of Israel and their relation with God. The people constantly refused to follow God. In 7:51, Stephen tells the people standing there that they resist the Holy Ghost, just as their ancestors did. In other words, they were resisting God. Stephen equates the Holy Ghost with God.

Through this brief look we can see that the Holy Spirit has been considered as God in both the Old Testament and the New Testament.

Quick Review

Within the whole Bible, both Old and New Testaments, God has given us a picture of His triune being. He has declared explicitly that He is a single entity, and that no one else is to infringe on that. While at the same time, He has shown that there are three distinct personages within this Entity.

This is the great mystery of God. There is one Entity, yet three distinct Beings. There is one mind, yet three unique personalities. Were these personalities not physical in nature, we could assume that God was suffering from multiple personality disorder. But these are physical beings with personalities. God is three in one, and one in three.

In the next section we will try to examine how the trinity operates. What other clues has God given us about this aspect of Himself?

The Trinity Examined

In the last section we started our study of the trinity by seeing that the Bible states God is a single entity, but at the same time proclaiming three beings as God. Now, we are going to go a little deeper and see if we can't find out more about each individual within the entity of God, and how they interact with each other.

God Progressively Reveals the Nature of the Trinity

There is a thing in the study of theology called "progressive revelation." This means that God only revealed certain aspects of His being or nature at certain times. He started with basic facts about Himself, and then added details later.

A good correlation to this is teaching a child to read. We begin with basics. We teach the child the letters of the alphabet. Then we show the child how those letters form words, then sentences and paragraphs, and, before we know it, they are reading books. A person can always read new books and learn new words, constantly deepening his knowledge of a language.

So it is with God. He has revealed a portrait of Himself to us over time. He began with a sketch and then filled in some colors and details. The closer we look at the portrait, the more details we will see about God.

Around the time of Moses people had a sketch of God. They knew some basic facts. Those who came later, around the time of King David and the prophets, had some of the details about God. When Jesus came, He presented more details to us. And now that we have the Holy Spirit to teach us, we can see even more intricate details. It has been, and continues to be a progression. When we get to heaven to live with God, we will see even more than we do now.

When it comes to revealing the trinity, God has revealed it progressively. Like a three sided jewel, God seemed to only reveal one side at a time, even though the whole is the jewel. This explains why the writers of the Old Testament did not distinguish between God the Father and the Holy Spirit. So, let us take a look at the progression of this revealing by God, and, at the same time, look a little closer at the characteristics of each person in the trinity.

God the Father

God revealed Himself to Moses as the God Moses' ancestors had worshipped. He made His presence known through a bush that was burning, but not consumed (Exodus 3:1-6). Right away God let it be known that He was unapproachable. He was unique and powerful. Moses was not to take God lightly.

God showed His power to Israel through the plagues He caused against the Egyptians (Exodus 7-12). He showed His intelligence by giving them the Ten Commandments (Exodus 20:1-17). When it came to the worship of God, He set some very strict boundaries. The sacrifices had to be performed in a certain way, by certain people, and at certain times. We read all these regulations in Leviticus.

God also chose to make His presence known on earth. He had the people construct a tabernacle while they were in the wilderness. This consisted of walls of fabric forming court yards, and a tent which housed the most sacred place. Within this most sacred area, God had the people place an ark made of wood overlaid with gold (Exodus 37:1-9). The stone tablets with the Ten Commandments were placed inside the ark, which was called the Ark of the Covenant. When everything was complete, the presence of God manifested itself over the ark, inside the tent. It was seen as a cloud by day, and a fire by night, and no one could go near it (Exodus 40:34-38).

Leviticus 16 gives us one of the greatest examples of how separated God was from the people. In this chapter we find the requirements for the Day of Atonement. One day a year the High Priest was to enter the most sacred place where the ark was, and perform a sacrifice for the sins of the people. The High Priest was the only one allowed to enter into the presence of God, and if he did one thing wrong, he would die. This was the only time anyone was able to get near to God at all.

Later, during the time of the prophets, God showed Himself as more of a father. He spoke directly to people who were not High Priest. In fact, most of the prophets had no connection with the priesthood of Israel. God became a little more accessible, but not to the people in general.

God the Son

The next step God took in revealing Himself was a huge one, and we do not fully understand how He did it. God became a man. He became one of His own creations.

Genesis chapter 3 tells us that Adam and Eve both sinned and were punished because of it. With this sin, death entered the world. An animal was killed to make clothes for the two humans. Death is the penalty we face for sin. Because there has to be death to pay the price for sin, God later establishes the animal sacrifice.

But, in Genesis, God gives a glimpse of something He would do to pay the price for the sin of humans once and for all. An animal's death could never equal the death of a human. The animal had not sinned, but it was made to pay the price for the sin of a human. The only thing that could totally pay the price for a human life is if a person could live a perfect life and then give himself as sacrifice for everyone else. In Genesis 3:15, God hints that this would happen. God tells the serpent that, from the seed of a woman, one would come to bruise his head.

It is interesting that the seed in verse 15 is the seed of a woman. Even in that day it was considered that the seed came from a man, not a woman. That is why the lines of ancestry would always be traced through the men. So, in saying this, God gives us a hint that only the woman would have a part in this child, not the man.

Isaiah 7:14 seems to follow up on this idea as God promises to send a sign to Israel. A virgin is to have a child. Remember, this was before the days of invitro-fertilization. We have already looked at Isaiah 9:6, which tells us that God was going to become a man. What better way for God to enter the world as a man than through the miracle of a virgin giving birth?

Matthew 1:18-23 and Luke 1:26-38 both relate that Mary, the mother of Jesus, was a virgin when she became pregnant with Jesus. We have watched modern science create embryos in test tubes and then implant them in a woman's womb. We can manipulate the DNA and make a clone. So, the fact that God was able to enter the human race through a virgin should not be as shocking to us as it was to those of the first century. God was able to create a human body for Himself, without the aid of a man.

God became the perfect man. Perfect does not mean genetically perfect, but morally perfect. Jesus was 100% God and 100% man. How is it possible to be a 200% person? Man has two parts. He has a physical part, which we call flesh. We can see it and touch it. In this part lies our senses which help us relate to the outside world. The other part is metaphysical, the soul/spirit. It is the part we cannot see, the part that makes the person an individual personality. I believe Jesus was 100% man in His flesh and emotions, and in His ability to feel tempted by everything around Him, just as we are. And, I believe the spirit part of Jesus was 100% God.

Our soul, which is a part of the metaphysical portion of man, is the deciding vote on what we depend on in our life. If we depend on our senses, we will look to the things of this world to satisfy us and to determine our values. But, if we depend on our spirit, we will look to God to satisfy us and determine our morals (Romans 8:1-11). The spirit of Jesus was God, because He is God. In His human form, He lived in complete dependence on His spirit, even though He struggled with all of the things coming at Him from the physical side (Hebrews 4:14-15). His physical side was fully submitted to His metaphysical side.

I believe Philippians 2:5-8 says it about as well as it can be said. Jesus, when He was in the form of God (the spirit form) was equal with God, He was God. When He became a man, He lived as a man should live, completely dependant on God. He actually placed Himself in our shoes and took on the role of a servant to God. He showed us what humans were to be like because He was the perfect human in relation to God. He obeyed God even to death. Jesus (God) was the one who lived the perfect life, never sinned, and then gave up His life as a sacrifice to pay for the sins of all humans (Hebrews 9:11-14).

With the advent of Jesus, God had gone from only letting His presence be known to one person, once a year, to walking and talking with the people of Israel face to face. But, His scope in human flesh was limited. He suffered all of the limitations we do in relating to people. He could only be in one place at a time, and could only cover a limited area. But, God's revelation of Himself had progressed. Details had been filled in.

We do not completely understand how God could be Jesus walking on earth, and still be the spirit being in heaven we refer to as the Father. But, as we have seen so far in this study, God's being is simply unimaginable to us. His human side was fully human while His spirit was completely in control of the universe with all the powers of the Deity.

The Holy Spirit

The final progression we see in the Bible of God revealing Himself to us is the Holy Spirit. The Holy Spirit was revealed in the Old Testament, but was mentioned and used sparingly. The Spirit only entered certain people at certain times, for specific purposes. When the purpose was completed the Spirit left that person, such as Samson in the book of Judges. Once the battle was over, the Spirit would leave Samson until needed again.

It is in the New Testament that we see the Holy Spirit living within, or indwelling, people permanently. It is recorded in Acts 1:8 that Jesus told the disciples that they would receive the Holy Spirit within them so that they could be witnesses for Jesus. This comes about in Acts 2:1-4 as about 120 followers of Jesus are gathered in a room. It was the day of Pentecost, a Jewish feast held 50 days after the feast of Firstfruits. The feast of Firstfruits was a part of the week long Passover celebration. Jesus was crucified during Passover. Suddenly, the room was filled with the sound a strong wind makes, a kind of roar, and little flames sat on top of each person in the room. The Holy Spirit had entered each person.

Paul tells us in Romans that we are to live according to the Spirit, and the Holy Spirit is in us if we have a relationship with Jesus (Romans 8:9,11). The Spirit dwells in us, or lives within us. This is a permanent arrangement.

In writing to the church of Corinth, Paul reminds them that they are the temple of God because the Holy Spirit lives in them (1 Corinthians 3:16). The early church knew that the indwelling of the Holy Spirit was not just a temporary, every-once-in-a-while, live-in arrangement. This was God permanently living within those who had a relationship with Him through Jesus.

God has now progressed from face-to-face in the flesh, and being limited, to living within each person who has a relationship with Jesus. All over the world people have God living within them. They are ordinary human beings, not God themselves, but they have the God living within them, in close relationship. Now God's presence is known to all who follow Him, instead of to one High Priest. His presence is there twenty four hours a day, seven days a week, instead of just once a year. God's presence is up close and personal instead of being hidden in a room in a temple. The Holy Spirit has completely transformed the way we interact with God.

It is important to note that the terms we use to distinguish between the members of the trinity are based partly on the fact of progressive revelation. We call Jesus the Son because we consider the God we cannot see or approach to be the Father. Jesus is not lower than the Father within the trinity, or the entity of God. It is just that Jesus was revealed second in progression, and in a visible form. We had to call Him something, and Son was the best fitting. It comes closest in our human language of describing the relationship between the two members.

A son is not lower than his father. A father is not human and a son sub-human. They are both humans and equal. But a son is to give respect to his father, and to humbly obey him. That is what Jesus did. He became a human, and then showed the respect to God that a human should. He honored and obeyed God humbly, just as a son would his father. Jesus did not become sub-God, He remained fully God.

The Holy Spirit is sometimes thought of as the least in the trinity because He was fully revealed last. The Spirit is God, and is not a lesser being just because He is last in line. It is the Holy Spirit that works directly within people. This makes Him the most intimate part of God, but no less powerful.

Jesus Reveals the Interaction of the Trinity

The Apostle John gives us an eyewitness testimony of the final teaching by Jesus to His disciples, right before He was arrested and crucified. Within this teaching Jesus speaks a lot about the relationship between the Father, Son, and Holy Spirit. Let us look at John 14-17 to see what Jesus had to tell His disciples.

Jesus makes a remarkable declaration in John 14:6. He states that He is the only way to get to the Father. Only through a relationship with Jesus can anyone come into the presence of God the Father. If we continue reading through to verse 14, we find that Jesus is asked by the disciples to show them the Father. He tells them that they have seen Him, so they have seen the Father. Jesus was saying, I am God in the flesh. He was equating Himself with the Father. They are one, yet separate.

Verses 15 through 24 expand the relationship within God further. Jesus now introduces the Holy Spirit. This will be a totally new concept for the disciples. Jesus states that He is going to leave them. They do not understand yet about the death, resurrection, and ascension of Jesus that will take place. But they do understand He is going to be with God. In order to comfort them as they consider the loss, Jesus tells them that, when He leaves, He will have the Father send the Holy Spirit to dwell in them (16,17). Then, He says that He will come to them (21). This makes Him the same as the Holy Spirit. By verse 23, Jesus states that The Father and Son will dwell in people. This makes all three persons of God living in a person through the Holy Spirit. They are all equal and the same.

At the end of verse 24 we seem to run into trouble. Jesus says that He was sent by the Father. He repeats this several times in His final teaching (16:5, 27-28; 17:3,8,18,21-23). So, if Jesus was sent, then He must be a different person than the Father right? Not necessarily. To be sent somewhere means that you had a specific purpose for coming. Jesus said earlier that His mission was to seek and to save those who are lost (Luke 19:10). He also came that the world might be saved

(John 3:17). Jesus came for the express purpose of dying to pay the price for our sin. He was sent.

In the passage in Luke 19, Jesus said that He came to accomplish a task. He was not sent; He came of His own free will. In His final teaching He says He was sent. Both are true. The collective trinity decided there was only one way to save humans from eternal death, and that was for God to become man. Collectively, God sent the Son to accomplish this mission. But Jesus was in on the process and volunteered.

John 14:26 shows us the mission of the Spirit. He is to help the disciples remember what Jesus taught. This mission statement is expanded in 16:8-14. The Spirit is to convince people of what is right and wrong, show us truth, and lead us into a deeper relationship with Jesus.

We have already touched on John 14:28. The Father is greater than the Son. In a sense this is true. In the human form Jesus was in, God the Father's spirit form was greater. It was more powerful, and more awesome than the human form the disciples saw in front of them. But, in essence, the two were the same.

Back in 14:16, Jesus said that the Father would send the Spirit to the disciples. In 15:26, Jesus says He will send the Spirit to the disciples. Once again, the Father and Son are considered separate, but still the same.

Following up on the previous thought, Jesus not only says that He will send the Spirit, but that the Spirit will not come unless Jesus leaves (16:7). As long as God the Son was in the world, there was not much need of having the Holy Spirit in the world at the same time. Jesus left so that the Spirit could do His work in believers.

There are a couple of times Jesus says the word proceeded, or came out of, the Father. The first is in reference to the Holy Spirit (15:26), and the second is in reference to the Son (16:27-28). Once again, this goes back to the sent question. You have three members of the trinity, which combined are God, and even separate are God. I believe the Father in these references is referring to the combined trinity. It would be much easier to talk to the disciples that way instead of having to fully define the trinity. If this is true, then what Jesus is saying is that the part of God that is the Son came from the Trinity, as did the Holy Spirit. Since God is the trinity, and the trinity is God, this would make sense.

After all of that, we realize that even Jesus could not explain the trinity of God using our language. But He does show that each part is interlocked with the other. Each person of the trinity is an individual in mission and personality, yet they are all one in being and mind. The Three are One, and the One is Three. It is simply incomprehensible, and makes me wonder why I ever started out to try to explain it in the first place. Actually I do know why, and that leads us to our brush strokes.

Brush Strokes

Within His final prayer with His disciples, Jesus prays that they would be one as He and the Father are one (John 17:11). He goes on to ask that all those who believe in Him would be one in the same way (17:21-23). Understanding the relationship between the Father and Son, and the Holy Spirit, should help us understand what Jesus wanted for us.

God is one entity in substance and mind. Yet, he is three beings who are individuals. Those who have a relationship with Jesus are bound together by the Holy Spirit living within them. We have a relationship with God. With that bond should be a singleness of heart and mind toward one another. We should have a loving relationship with all other believers.

The trinity is all about relationship. We are many people, yet we are united as one in God. We are individuals, but we should all be headed the same direction in our thoughts and lives. Jesus knows the joy of intimate relationship with the other members of the trinity, and He wants us to experience that kind of relationship amongst ourselves.

The prayer of Jesus was for those who believed in Him, who would enter into a relationship with Him. But, Jesus came to save the world. Even though not everyone will accept Jesus into their life, it was a part of the original plan. Every human was supposed to know that kind of relationship.

Adam and Eve in the garden had that kind of relationship. Genesis 2:25 tells us that Adam and Eve were naked, and were not ashamed. I don't believe this is a reference to sex. What this verse is telling us is that these two people had absolutely no secrets from each other. They knew each other intimately emotionally, mentally, spiritually, and yes, even physically.

This intimacy in relationships is what God had planned all along. It is what every person in the world seeks, even if they don't know it or won't admit it. It is the need to know and be known. To have someone you can be completely open with and share everything. This is more of a matter for the heart, soul, and mind, than it is of the body.

Jesus prayed that each believer would have this intimacy of being one with each other. We know He was not talking physically because He was with all guys. So, the deep level of oneness must come from the other areas, the spiritual, emotional, and mental. Everyone who has a relationship with Jesus should be able to experience this with every other believer.

Unfortunately, the church is not made up of perfect people. (Or perhaps that is fortunate since I would not be allowed in if perfection was a requirement.) Because we are not perfect, we cannot truly achieve the closeness Jesus desired while we are here on earth, but I believe that those who are in Jesus have a better shot than those who do not. I have seen that when believers allow God to lead them, that they can have an extremely open relationship with other believers. As the believers rely on the same Spirit, they gain the same attitude toward each other. It is as if they are of the same mindset. It is hard work, and we must trust in God for help. But, it must be important because Jesus prayed for us to be one. I believe it helps to remember that Jesus is still praying for us to love each other and be one, just as the Trinity is One.

God Is Eternal/Self-Existent

Imagine that there has never been a time when you were not reading this book. There was never a time when you started reading; you have just always been reading it. Then imagine that there will never be a time when you are not reading this book. Believe me it isn't really that long, but just imagine that it never ends. That is what it means to be eternal; never beginning, never ending, always being.

God is Eternal.

As a spirit being there has never been a time when God did not exist. There will never be a time when He ceases to exist. When we speak of existence, we are referring to a conscious, living existence. Dinosaur bones exist, but the dinosaur does not. God has always been a living entity, fully conscious and active.

Before Moses died he pronounced a blessing on the tribes of Israel. Within that blessing Moses declares that God is eternal (Deuteronomy 33:27). Even in His earliest communications with the Jews God revealed this concept of Himself.

Psalm 90 relates how God being eternal has an effect on people who are not eternal. In verse two it is said that God is God from everlasting to everlasting, in other words, eternity. There has never been, and never will be, a time when God is not God. Paul states the same concept in 1 Timothy 1:17, when he quotes from a benediction used by the early church.

Perhaps the most powerful statement in the Bible declaring God as eternal comes from the book of Revelation. Chapter four brings us into the very throne room of God in heaven. The Apostle John, who is relating what he sees, tells us that there is a throne, and that God is on the throne. There are four beasts and twenty four elders surrounding the throne, and they are giving praise and worship to God. Among their statements of truth about God in their praise is that God "was, and is, and is to come." And He is the One who lives for ever and ever (Revelation 4:8-10).

These two statements, but especially the first, declare God to be eternal. He was; He has always existed. He is; He exists now. He is to come; He will always exist. God has no time boundaries. He will live forever and ever; He will never cease to exist. God was never born, He will never die. That is eternal.

God Must Be Self-Existent

Being eternal and being self-existent go hand in glove. One cannot be true without the other. A being must be eternal in order to be considered self-existent, and must be self-existent in order to be considered eternal. Therefore, in order to be eternal there must have never been a time when God was not in existence. God could not have been created, or spontaneously entered into being. In order for this to be true God must, of necessity, be self-existent. A being could never be eternal who was not self-existent.

To be self-existent means that God does not rely on anyone or anything for His existence. We had to rely on our parents for our existence. Plants have to rely on a seed, and animals have to rely on their parents. But God was not generated from a parent or a seed. He existed. God has no ancestor, no progenitor.

God declared His self-existence when He introduced Himself to Moses from the burning bush. Moses asked what God's name was, so He could tell the Hebrews which God was leading them out of Egypt. After all, there were many gods in Egypt. God said "I Am that I Am." Tell the people that I Am sent you Moses (Exodus 3:13, 14). That is a strong statement of self-existence. God exists because He exists, not because men dreamed Him up, or because creation needed a God to run things. He was not born from a higher God, or a lesser god. He is real. He exists solely because His being is to exist.

God is complete and perfect in His essence to the point that He needs no outside assistance in order to live. "I Am that I Am" is the complete package. Nothing needs to be added, and nothing can be taken away. His existence is pure, untouchable, and undiminished.

We need to eat food, drink water and breathe air in order to continue our existence. God needs nothing to continue His. God's eternality would be threatened if He had to rely on anything to sustain His existence. For instance, if God had to rely on air to breathe in order to remain alive, He would suffocate and die if the air were gone. This would end His existence. God cannot rely on anything else for His existence.

Because God is self-existent He can give life to other beings. We can give blood, or maybe an organ, but God can give life. He is pure life, and can infuse inanimate matter with life in order to make it alive. We see this in the first chapters of the Bible. God did not create lifeless, sculptured animals and plants; He infused life into every living thing. Like us donating a little blood, God can donate life and not diminish Himself.

Genesis 2:7 tells us that God breathed life into man. He took man, formed him from the dust of the earth, and then gave him life. This was not mouth-to-mouth resuscitation like we do to revive a drowning victim. This was breathing life into something that had never lived before. It would be like us taking a rock and making it come alive. Chapter 1 of Genesis shows us that God created all the animals from inanimate matter, and then gave them life. The plants are the same way. Nothing would be alive, plant or animal, if God had not placed life in it.

This answers one of the basic questions we have about the existence of our universe. How did lifeless, inanimate matter produce living plants, animals and people? God donated life to them.

The giving of life to certain parts of creation makes this world a zoo instead of a museum. In a museum you have lifeless paintings, statues, and maybe some machinery to look at. They are all dead representations. There is no interaction between the exhibits and those looking at them. But in a zoo, you have living creatures that interact with those who have come to see and enjoy them.

God's purpose in giving us life was so that He could enjoy us, and we could interact with Him. He wanted us to have an eternal relationship with Him, so He gave us a life like His own which will last forever. God gave us plants and animals so that we might enjoy their presence. How boring this world would be if people were the only things living in it. Just think how much fun it would be to live on the moon.

The Son Must Be Pre-Existent

If God is eternal, then all three parts of God must be eternal. This means that Jesus, the Son, would have had to have existed before the conception in Mary took place. If the Son did not come into being until that time, then it means He was created, not self-existing, and not eternal. The body of Jesus, the human form the Son took, was created at the time of conception. But what we want to look at is the God part, the spirit part, of Jesus having existed prior to His arrival in human form. What evidence can we find for this from the picture God has given us in the Bible?

On the night He was betrayed by Judas and led away to face trial and death on the cross, Jesus prayed a prayer with His remaining disciples. This prayer is recorded in John 17. We have already looked at part of that prayer when we discussed the trinity of God and the oneness of believers. But earlier in the prayer

Jesus makes this statement: "Father, You glorify me with Your glory, the same way You glorified me when I was with you before the world existed." That is a rough paraphrase of verse 5.

The key thought of that verse is that Jesus existed before the world existed. We know the human form had not existed until coming into this world through Mary. So, it is the God part of Jesus which existed with the Father, even before creation.

It is in his letter to the Philippians that Paul confronts the fact that Jesus pre-existed His earthly form. Philippians 2:6-7 tells us that Jesus was in the form of God, in other words He was God, and then He became a man to walk this earth.

We have considered John 8:58 before as we looked at Jesus declaring He was God. In this passage He states that He was before Abraham, as well as declaring He is God.

So, we can see clearly that Jesus existed prior to His conception in Mary. This gives us one of the necessities for being able to state with certainty that Jesus is eternal. But with John 8:58, Jesus declares that He is the I AM. This leads us to the next thing that must be true of Jesus if we are to know for sure that He is eternal, not just a creation of God.

The Son Must Be Self-Existent

In order to be eternal, Jesus must be self-existent. Remember, nothing can be eternal without being self-existent, and nothing can be self-existent without being eternal. God gave His great I Am name to Moses at the burning bush to identify Himself and His nature. Jesus used the same statement in John 8:58 to identify Himself. By declaring that name for Himself, Jesus declared the truth of that name as applying to Him. In other words Jesus was saying that everything that is true about God, which is implied by this name, is true about me. As we discussed, I AM is a statement of self-existence. Jesus declared Himself to be self-existent.

That would be enough evidence, but God goes on to press the issue in other parts of the New Testament. Hebrews 1:2-3, tells us that Jesus had a part in creation, and that everything is held together with His power. Paul goes further in Colossians 1:16-17. He says that everything was created by Jesus, and nothing exists without Him.

What are the implications of those two passages? Well, if Jesus created everything, then He created both the inanimate objects, and the living creatures. In order to say He created living creatures, He would have had to have been the one who gave them life. Only a self-existing being can donate life to an inanimate object to make it live. This would be clear evidence that Jesus was self-existent.

In thinking about Jesus donating life as being proof of self-existence, I began to see a familiar portion of scripture differently. John chapter 1 took on a new light for me. In this chapter the Apostle John is giving us an introduction to Jesus. He begins with Jesus' pre-existence when he says that the Word (Jesus) was in the beginning with God, and was God (vs. 1,2).

But, John does not leave it there. The next verse, verse three, says that everything was made by Him. This is the creation evidence for self-existence. But, verse four is the one that floors me. It says that in Him, Jesus, was life, and this life was the light of men. This is a clear declaration that Jesus is life itself; not just spiritually but physically. Jesus, the self-existent being had life in Himself, which He gave to men. God breathed life into Adam (Genesis 2:7).

Could John have made any clearer declaration to the Deity of Jesus? With just a few well chosen words John declares that Jesus was pre-existent and self-existent. Those are the two qualifications needed for Jesus to be eternal.

In case there is still any doubt, Jesus declares Himself to be eternal in Revelation 1:11,17,18. He is the beginning and the end. In other words, He has always existed, and always will.

The Holy Spirit Must Be Eternal In Existence

Hebrews 9:14 states that the Spirit is eternal. But, it is never good to base a belief on just a single verse of scripture. Other scriptures must support this belief. The fact that the Holy Spirit is God is reason to believe that He is eternal, since God is eternal. But, can we find other evidence for this?

Let us look at the evidence for the self-existence of the Holy Spirit. If the Spirit is self-existent, then He is also eternal. We know that the Spirit was involved in creation of the universe. Genesis 1:2 tells us He was present. Job declares that the Spirit gave him life (Job 33:4). David talks about the fish of the ocean and how they are totally dependent on God to take care of them. He concludes with the fact that God can take the breath from them and they will die, but, His Spirit gives them life in the first place (Psalm 104:30).

The Holy Spirit, by His activity in creation and giving life, is self-existent, and therefore eternal. Malachi 2:10 clearly states that we were created by one God.

Since we have already determined that the Holy Spirit is God, we know for certain that He, the Son, and the Father are all self-existent, and all eternal.

Conclusion

It is important that God is eternal. Why would we want to follow a God who is here one day and gone the next? God will always be here, as He has always been here. He is self-existent so He does not have to depend on anything for His existence. We do not have to worry that God will lack something and die because it is not there. He is able to give us life, and surround us with life. Because of Him all things exist, and without Him nothing could continue existing.

Brush Strokes

There are at least three things we can learn about ourselves from the fact that God is eternal and self-existent.

We are dependent beings

As much as we like to think of ourselves as being independent, we are not. God is self-existent and therefore fully independent of everything and everyone. When we think about it we realize that we are fully dependent beings, quite the opposite of God.

We rely on our parents for conception, and our mother for birth. If someone did not take care of us for the first few years of our life, we would not survive. We are dependent on air to breath, water to drink, and food to eat. Doctors are needed when we have medical problems, along with the medicines they provide. We are a dependent and needy species.

Whether we want to admit it or not, God is the one we have to rely on most in our lives. He is the one who provides us with life in the first place. God is the source of life, and there is nothing living that did not get its life from God. He created the earth and all we see. The sun for warmth, the moon for beauty, the plants and animals for food, were all created by Him. God holds everything together through His power (Hebrews 1:2-3).

Physically, everything we have is provided by God. We may think that we work for what we get, that we provide for ourselves, but this is simply not true. We may work to get money to pay for food, but where did the food come from in the first place? God gave life to the plants and animals so we could have that food.

We can buy a car, or a house, but where did the steel and lumber come from? God provided life to the people to build, He gave them skills in which to build, and He provided al the raw materials needed. We work, yes, but God provides so we can. He is the one who gives us health and strength and abilities in order to work.

We have to face it. We are completely dependent on God for everything we have physically. And, we are dependent on Him for everything we need spiritually.

God's purpose of relationship

God created us with a spiritual side. When God created Adam and Eve, He wanted to make them in His own image (Genesis 1:26, 27). As we discussed in the first chapter, the image of God is spirit. It is formless. So, if God is going to make people in His own image, He must be placing within them a spirit of their own. By doing this God intentionally set humans apart from the other creatures of creation.

But why would God do this? God wanted to have a relationship with us. By placing a spirit within each person, God, a spirit being, is able to communicate and have a relationship with each person. Our spirit speaks with His Spirit (Romans 8:16). God's plan for humanity is to have a relationship with each and every person.

Genesis chapter three relates the tragedy of Adam and Eve. They were perfect in physical form, and even in spirit. They lived in a perfect world. They only had one rule to follow; do not eat of a certain tree (2:16, 17). Eve was deceived into eating the fruit, but Adam willfully ate of it. Both disobeyed God. This disobedience was called sin.

Sin caused a separation between people and God. Knowing they had done wrong, Adam and Eve hid from God. Then, God forced them out of the garden. Evil had entered into the human race like a plague against body and spirit. This evil, or sin, caused people to not be able to communicate or have a relationship with God as was intended. It brought death to the physical body and a death of the spirit through separation from God.

Believe it or not, God knew this was going to happen, even before He created Adam and Eve. His plan to reclaim the relationship with people was already in motion. As we discussed in the last chapter when talking about God the Son, God had already decided to take on human form, live a perfect life as a man, and then die to pay the price for the sin of humanity. This was the only way to regain the spiritual relationship between God and people.

God has done everything for us spiritually in order for us to have a relationship with Him. He has paid the price for us. Therefore, just as we are physically dependent on Him, we are spiritually dependent on Him for everything.

There is a specific reason God made us with a spirit. The spirit part of us lasts forever. It will last as long as God lasts. We are not eternal, but we are everlasting. God wanted our relationship with Him to last forever. He did not want it to be just during the few years we live here on earth.

A changed world view

Paul spoke of life after death in 1 Corinthians chapter 15. He is defending the resurrection of Jesus, and says that if Jesus was not raised, then there is no life after death. But, He was raised, and therefore we can look forward to a life after this one. He repeats the same thought in 1 Thessalonians 4:13-18, and tells the people that we will always be with God after this life. This should be a comfort to everyone who has a relationship with God.

When we look in the book of Revelation we see that there are two types of people. There are those who have a relationship with God, and those who have refused to have a relationship with God.

Those who have accepted their dependence on Jesus, and His sacrifice for them, in establishing a relationship with God, will spend eternity with God. This relationship must be established while still alive on this earth. Once established, the relationship is eternal.

But, there are those who do not accept their dependence on Jesus. They do not want God to run their life. God allows these people to have what they want, even in eternity. Revelation 20:11-15 tells of the judgment of these people. The work they did during life is brought out for them to see. It proves that they wanted no part of God in running their life. Therefore, God places them for eternity in a place where He does not make His presence known. We call the place hell, it is really the Lake of Fire, and it is a horrible place because God does not let His goodness be present there. But, those people decided that they did not want God in their life. God simply gave them what they wanted.

Since there is life after death, how should that affect the way we live here? First, we should be preparing for life after death. We should establish our relationship with God while we have time right now. Do not put it off for another day; you never know when death is going to pull your name. And don't just stop with entering into a relationship. Grow in the relationship. This earth is just a training ground, an elementary school if you will, for preparing to spend eternity with God.

Second, we should view the things we possess as temporary. As they say, you can't take it with you. All of these possessions will be left behind when you die. So, maybe there are more important things to worry about in life instead of how much money, or how many toys we have. How do we treat others? Do we give to those who are less fortunate? Have we made the life of those around us better? These are the important things. Having wealth is fine, but what are you doing with it?

Finally, knowing that our bodies die here, but our spirit lives on should help us view death differently. We will always grieve the separation that comes with death. That is a must. But, if we know that the person had a relationship with God, then we can be comforted by the fact that they are with Him now.

If we have a relationship with God, then we should not fear death. We can be afraid of it being painful, but we should never fear what lies beyond our ability to see. However, if you do not have a relationship with God, then perhaps you should be fearful of what awaits you when you leave this earthly body.

Conclusion

This world is just a beginning to our journey of everlasting life. How we deal with God here effects where we end up spending eternity. We will either be with God, or separated from Him. It's our choice. Everything we see before us is temporary, but the things we cannot see last forever. This has to have an impact on our priorities in life, and our view of death.

God Is Everywhere Present/Immense

So far the picture we have of God is that He is way beyond us. He is an invisible spirit, a trinity, and eternally self-existent. God does not need us to survive. With this picture we might get the idea that God has nothing to do with us now, that He is aloof and uncaring, or that He simply keeps to Himself somewhere way beyond our reach or sight. Is it any wonder that we often ask the question, "Are you there God?"

While it is true that God is beyond anything we can honestly imagine; it is not true that He is aloof and far away. This next characteristic of God will show us exactly how close He really is to us. The portrait of God we find in the Bible shows us that He is present everywhere, all the time. The technical word for this is omnipresence. "Omni" means all, and when connected with presence, means that God is all, or everywhere, present.

God develops this part of His portrait in Jeremiah 23:23-24. He begins by asking if He is a God who is far off, out of touch. The answer is no. He is right there at hand. He is conscious of everything that is going on. He is present wherever people try to hide from Him. He sees them and knows what they are doing.

That is omnipresence. God is physically and consciously present everywhere, all at one time. Like the rest of God's features, this one is hard to understand. All of God is present everywhere at the same time. To use an anthropomorphism, His head is not one place and His foot another. He is not disseminated throughout the universe; He is fully in all places at the same time.

Some people try to make God everything. They say He is the tree, the rock, the air, the sun. This is called pantheism and it could not be further from what the Bible teaches. From the very first words of the Bible we see that God is separate from His creation. So, while God is present everywhere with His whole being, He is not everything.

God continues to describe Himself in the Jeremiah passage as filling heaven and earth. This speaks of God's immensity. Immensity means that God's physical being has no boundaries. It is different than omnipresence because immensity only deals with God's physical being, whereas omnipresence deals with His conscious presence as well as physical.

We always see things as having physical boundaries. The ocean has a boundary. Our atmosphere has a boundary. This solar system and even this galaxy have boundaries. We will probably discover some day that even this universe has a boundary. But God does not have any boundaries to His being. He is limitless.

Not only is God not bound by physical boundaries, meaning distance, He is also not bound by temporal boundaries, meaning time. Apparently God can be present in all times at the same time. The example of this is the book of Revelation.

The Apostle John, who wrote the book, was told to come up to heaven where God would show him what the future held (Revelation 4:1). While John is there he sees the last days of this world played out before him. He sees the final judgments of all people, and the beginning of the eternal state we will live in forever. John has to use descriptive words in order to try to describe what he is seeing, but this is not a dream, or a vision. He is seeing the actual events as they happened. God has actually propelled him into the future.

But, while John was in the future, the people of his time still existed. God had not abandoned that time period, and yet He was present in the future as well. God's omnipresence spans all time. I know, like everything else we have studied so far, this is mind blowing. Like television, I don't understand how it works, I just know it does.

The Father

In the Old Testament, God makes reference to His immensity and omnipresence. We have already looked at the passage in Jeremiah, so let us look at some other references. God declares in Isaiah 66:1 that heaven is His throne, and the earth is His footstool. This is a reference to His immensity. How big God must be if the whole earth is nothing more than a footstool to Him. Of course God is speaking figuratively. The earth could no more be an actual footstool to Him than a grain of sand could be a footstool for us.

Amos was an Old Testament prophet. God was speaking to him one day, telling him about the destruction he was going to bring on the people of Israel (Amos 9:2-4). To paraphrase what God is telling Amos, "You can run, but you can't hide." God is speaking of His omnipresence. He is conscious of everything that goes on. He is present everywhere these people might run to try to hide from Him.

God is the best source we can have in developing this picture of Him, but others in the Old Testament have also made statements concerning this aspect of God. In Isaiah we see some angels called seraphim standing before God, who has made His presence known in the temple in Jerusalem. They cry out that God's glory fills the whole earth (Isaiah 6:3). This speaks of God's omnipresence as He fills the whole earth with His physical and conscious presence.

King David wanted to build a temple for God, a place where the Ark of the Covenant would reside permanently. But God did not allow David to build the temple. Instead, David's son, Solomon, built it. At its dedication, Solomon offered a prayer to God in which he stated that heaven, and the heavens of heavens, could not hold God, and this temple could definitely not hold Him (1 Kings 8:27; 2 Chronicles 6:18). But Solomon believed that God would make His presence known in that sacred place. Solomon understood the immensity of God as it related to space. God can never be placed in a box.

Perhaps Solomon learned about the immensity and omnipresence of God from his father David. Psalm 139 records David's musings, or meditations, on two aspects of God. We will cover the other aspect in the next chapter, but, for now, let us look at verses 7-12. These are the verses that show us that David believed God to be omnipresent. There was nowhere David could go and be away from the presence of God. He was not trying to run away from God. David was finding comfort in the fact that God was with him no matter where he went.

In verses 11 and 12, David was finding satisfaction that God was with him even when times were hard, and darkness covered him emotionally. Have you ever been at a point in your life where everything just seemed dark? You could not see any light at the end of the tunnel, not even an approaching train. David had been there. He realized that not even that emotional darkness could keep God away. God was still there physically and consciously.

There is no doubt that God the Father is immense and omnipresent. He has no boundaries to His physical being. He is fully aware of all that goes on, no matter where it is, or when it takes place.

The Son

It is a given that the physical, human form of God the Son was not omnipresent. Flesh cannot be everywhere at once. It is confined to a single area. But, does this mean that Jesus was not omnipresent while on earth? Was He, or is He now, omnipresent? If He is God, then He is omnipresent.

One of the characteristics of being omnipresent is that you know what is going on wherever you are. You are aware, and acknowledge, everything that happens around you. (We call this being all knowing, and we will discuss it in detail in the next chapter.) In other words, if Jesus was omnipresent, He could be there with someone under a tree, even though the physical body of Jesus was a long way from the tree. Jesus would still know who that person was, and what he said and did.

We find an example of this in John 1:43-50. As Jesus was setting about to call His disciples, He came across Philip and asked him to follow along. Philip then went to find Nathaniel. Now, when Philip found Nathaniel he was sitting under a tree. Philip convinces Nathaniel to come meet Jesus. As Nathaniel approaches, Jesus greets him as an Israelite who was not at all deceitful. Apparently Nathaniel prided himself on his honesty. He asked Jesus how He knew him. Jesus tells Nathaniel that He saw him under the tree before Philip asked him to come. There must have been a long distance from where Jesus was to that tree because it impressed Nathaniel that Jesus had seen him.

The key word is "saw". Jesus did not say "I knew you were under a tree." Nor did He quip, "I felt that you were under a tree." Jesus was not in any way trying to pull a magicians trick, or pretend to be a psychic. He was telling Nathaniel that He had physically seen him under that tree. That is a statement that at least merits being in two places at once, if it doesn't show omnipresence.

But, there is another example which comes from three different Gospel writers. Matthew, Mark and John all three record the same event. It is arguably one of the best known miracles Jesus performed. He walked on water. But, do you know the particulars of the story?

Jesus had finished feeding the crowd of over five thousand people with only a few loaves of bread and some fish. He told His disciples to get into a boat and cross the Sea of Galilee while He sent the people away. After the disciples and the people left, Jesus went up to a mountain to pray.

While there are some differences in the narratives, the basic facts are the same, and there are no discrepancies (Matthew 14:22-32; Mark 6:45-51; John 6:15-21). Around three to six in the morning hours, Jesus looked out on the Sea of Galilee and, according to Mark, saw the disciples straining to row against the heavy wind. Now, Jesus was on a mountain which would extend His line of sight. But, it was dark, and John tells us that the disciples were a good three to four miles out. Also take into account the heavy waves around them, and there is no way Jesus could have actually seen them with human eyes.

Forget for a moment that Jesus walked the three to four miles on the water to get to the boat where the disciples were. He saw them when it was not humanly possible to do so. Could this not be taken as at least circumstantial evidence that Jesus was omnipresent, even though He was in human form?

Toward the end of His ministry Jesus made two statements to His disciples which show us that He is omnipresent. The first is found in Matthew 18:20. Jesus declares that wherever two or three people are gathered together to worship Him, He is there with them. This means that anywhere in the world where at least two people are gathered to worship Jesus, He will be right there with them.

Jesus was not talking figuratively here. Sometimes we will tell someone that our thoughts will be with them. That is not what Jesus was saying. We will also hear people say that if you think about a lost loved one, it is like they are there with you. That was not what Jesus was talking about either. He was saying that He will be physically present with those who are worshipping Him. Not only would He be physically present, but He would also be consciously present, actively participating in the group.

Obviously at any one time on this earth there are hundreds, or thousands, of such groups meeting to worship Jesus, especially on Sunday mornings. So, how could Jesus be in all those places at one time if He was not omnipresent? This declaration of Jesus was a statement of His deity, and His ability to be everywhere at once.

We must remember that the Son is 100% human, which means that the physical part of Jesus, the body, was restricted here on earth. But, He is also 100% God, which means He is unrestricted spirit. When Jesus attends a meeting it is as an active participant with those who are there. He is listening to their prayers, and acting on them. Jesus hears the praise given to God and soaks it in. He touches hearts, minds, and lives as the people worship in His name. An immense God could have part of Himself present, but an omniscient God has all of Himself consciously present at each and every meeting all over the earth.

After His resurrection Jesus met with His disciples on a mountain in Galilee (Matthew 28:16-20). There He commanded them to be witnesses for Him throughout the world. With His last words He promises them that He will always be with them, even to the end of the world.

We have already talked about Jesus being eternal. This promise has a definite time factor involved with it. Jesus is going to be with those who believe in Him all the way to the end of time on this earth. But, it also has a space factor. The previous promise was for groups of people. This promise is for individuals. Jesus is going to be with each individual believer wherever they are in the world. The only way He could accomplish this is to be omnipresent.

If Jesus was not omnipresent, then a lot of people's praise and worship would be wasted. Prayers would simply fall into a void of stale air instead of on the ears of God. But Jesus is present and active when people gather to pray to Him. He is there when a person calls on His name for help. He is listening, and acting on those prayers. He feels the love given to Him by praise, and returns that love to those who praise Him.

It is hard to understand how Jesus can be omnipresent. We think of Him in His human form and we just do not see how it is possible. But, Jesus is God, and nothing is impossible for God. He can be with a small group of believers in China, a missionary in Brazil, and a single mother in the United States kneeling to pray for her sick child, all at the same time.

The Holy Spirit

The Holy Spirit, being the Spirit of God, is as immense as God. But, is the Holy Spirit omnipresent? Let's look again at Psalm 139:7. David asks specifically, where he can go from God's Spirit. The Holy Spirit is present everywhere, just like the Father.

We saw that Jesus is able to be with believers all over the world at the same time. The same is true for the Holy Spirit. The Apostle Paul has something to say about that.

In 1 Corinthians 3:16 and 6:19, Paul is talking to the Christians in Corinth. He tells them that their body is the temple, or dwelling place, of the Holy Spirit. This is true of each individual Christian. The Holy Spirit lives inside each person who has a relationship with God through Jesus. This is true no matter where in the world they may be. So, right now, millions of people have the Holy Spirit residing in them.

This is not a case of a piece, or part, of the Spirit being given to each person. The whole, conscious Spirit lives within each person. He enters in and sets up housekeeping. Paul states in Romans 8:9 that if the Spirit does not live in someone they do not have a relationship with God. But he goes on from there to describe some of the things the Spirit does within a person. In other words, he shows that the whole Spirit is alive and active within the person.

The Spirit gives us life (Romans 8:10-13). It is a strong spiritual life that is at the core of our being. This is what the Spirit energizes within us to make us alive.

The flesh, our body, already has life. But our spirit is dead, unanimated, until the Holy Spirit shows up to jump start it.

The Holy Spirit leads us (Romans 8:14). He shows us right and wrong, and directs us in the way God wants us to go in our life. He confirms to us that we are in right relationship with God (Romans 8:16). When we are not sure how to pray; He will pray with and for us (Romans 8:26). He knows our deepest need, even better than we do (Romans 8:27).

Paul wrote to another church in Galatia. In that letter he lists the fruit of the Spirit: love, joy, peace, patience, gentleness, goodness, faith, meekness, temperance (Galatians 5:22-23). All of these are active qualities of a person's life. They are not passive, they all have to be acted out, or acted on. It is the Spirit who helps the person develop these qualities in their life.

The Spirit is not passive when He enters a person's life to set up housekeeping. He is working hard within each and every individual in whom He resides. This demonstrates the quality of omnipresence. Not only is He living within millions of people at once, but He is active and participating within their life. He is conscious of their need, and takes action to help. This means that all of the Spirit resides within each and every person who has a relationship with God through Jesus.

Brush Strokes

It is quite obvious that we are not omnipresent. Although some parents of small children and teens wish they could be in two places at once sometimes, it just is not going to happen. We are not immense either. We take up space, but we have specific boundaries. So, how does God being omnipresent relate to us?

When David asked in Psalm 139 where he could go to be away from God's presence, he was not looking for an escape route. He was looking for comfort. It was a comfort to him that no matter where he was on earth, God would be there. God was not confined to the box called the Ark of the Covenant. He was not even confined to the borders of Israel. Anywhere David went, God would be there.

There is also an aspect where David is saying, "No matter how bad a situation may become, God is there." Verses 11 and 12 give us David's thoughts about depression, and hard times. When everything in your life goes dark, God is there. When the darkness seems to hide God from us, we are never hidden from God.

There is an old adage, "There are no atheists in foxholes." In other words, when times are hard, people look at God. The deeper the crises, whether individual, or national, the more prone people are to look at God.

Some people, like David, look to God for comfort. They realize that He is still there for them, even during the time of extreme pain. Others look to God in order to blame Him for what has happened. But both sets of people realize that God is omnipresent, and that He is there. We are not going to get into the question of why God allows bad things to happen. That is a subject for another time. Right now we want to just focus on the fact that God is there, no matter how we are reacting to Him.

David acknowledges that God is there in the good times as well. Many of the Psalms are praises to God for being there during a rough time, but others are about God being there in a time of joy. Psalm 139:9 talks about taking flight with the wings of the dawn. We could interpret that as being a time of extreme joy. God is not just there when we are in trouble, but He is there when we are having a good time as well.

It seems that crises make us think about God's presence, and good times make us forget it. Face it, when everything is running smoothly we don't even think about God being present. But, the minute something goes wrong, we wonder where He is.

It is like electricity. I come into my house and flip on the light switch without giving a thought to the electricity that runs the light. I don't think about the workers at the power company who are working hard so that the electricity will reach my house and I can have lights. But, when, for some reason, the electricity goes off, that is all I can think about. Where are those people? Why haven't they fixed my electricity? When is it going to come back on?

We tend to focus more on God when we are in distress than when we are happy. But, God is always there for us. He is omnipresent. There is no place He cannot be. This should be a source of comfort for us.

We cannot be with a family member who is in harms way fighting a war, but God is. We cannot be with that new teenage driver as they go solo for the first time, but God is. We may not be able to be with a sick relative who is in the hospital, but God is. God is there for scraped knees and home runs, first dates and rejections, weddings and funerals. In every part of our life God is there and He is active.

This is one of those times when we must humbly acknowledge that God is far above us, and accept the fact that we need Him to be omnipresent. We are confined in this body to being in one place at one time. We cannot always be with those we want to comfort, or celebrate with those who are happy. But we can rest assured that God is with them. As for us, there is no corner too dark, no depression too deep, no joy too ecstatic, no place too high or too far where God can be left behind.

God Knows Everything

To say that God is smart, or that He is intelligent, is a gross understatement. The Bible paints a portrait of a God who knows everything there is to know. This characteristic is directly linked to omnipresence. Because God is physically and consciously present everywhere, He knows what is going on. But, it goes deeper than just a cursory knowledge of events. Like everything else about God, this gets complicated. God knows about everything we can see, and everything that is invisible. He knows everything that has happened, is happening, and will happen. He even knows the possibilities of what could happen, and which choices will be made.

God simply knows everything there is to know. The fancy word for this is omniscient. "Omni" means "all," and "science" means "knowledge." God has all knowledge.

The Father

Let us begin by looking at the way God the Father is described in the Old and New Testaments.

God knows how creation is put together because He created it.

A master craftsman can tell you the name of each and every part of the machine he built. He can also tell you what the purpose is of each pulley, cog and lever. He can quote the specs for the size or dimension of each part. The craftsman knows what he has designed and built. Could we expect God to be any different?

Once again we must refer back to the very first words of the Bible which tell us specifically that God created the universe (Genesis 1:1). In order to create the universe, God had to plan it out. He did not just haphazardly throw it together and hope for the best. He had a clearly planned out design.

And, because He designed it, and built it, He knows how and why everything works. He knows each component and part. We are still discovering how everything fits together, or what it is made of. But, God already knows these things, down to the minutest detail.

We do not even know exactly how many stars are in this galaxy, not to mention the entire universe. But, Psalm 147:4-5, tells us that God knows exactly how many stars compose this universe, and even knows the name of each one. In Isaiah 40:26, God states again that He knows the name of each star. God has named all the stars. That is attention to detail. The fact that He remembers the names of countless stars is amazing to me. I have trouble remembering the names of people I meet; I can't imagine remembering all of the names of the stars.

Verse 5 of the Psalm tells us that God's understanding, or knowledge, is infinite. Just as there is no limit to His being, there are no boundaries to His knowledge. As we will see, God's knowledge extends beyond just how creation works, or what it consists of.

The book of Job is the poetic recitation of one man's struggle with understanding God. Maybe you have heard the phrases "poorer than Job's turkey", or "the trials of Job." These are references to this Biblical character. To make a long story short, the Reader's Digest way, God allowed Job to be wiped out and then built him up again better than he was before. The book of Job chronicles Job's puzzlement over God letting him suffer. Job had always followed God and believed in Him, but he lost his whole fortune and entire family, except for his wife, all in one day. Then, he became very ill.

Job contemplates all this and, as we go through the book, basically demands an audience with God to have Him explain Himself. In other words, Job wanted his day in court because He did not understand how God could be that unfair. For thirty seven chapters Job and his friends try to figure this thing out. His friends always came up with the wrong conclusion, and Job always wanted to speak directly to God to question Him.

Finally, in chapter 38, God shows up and begins to speak with Job. But, it does not go as Job anticipated. Instead of Job asking the questions of God, God asks the questions of Job. Within this interrogation by God in chapters 38 and 39, are some really good points about the knowledge and intelligence God has.

God's first question to Job was, "Do you know how the earth is designed?" Right away Job is silenced, and just has to listen as God lays out all the things He does in creation. He placed limits on the waters to keep them in the ocean. He causes the dawn every morning. God knows what exists at the bottom of the ocean. He causes it to rain, even where no one else is around, just so the plants can live.

God continues to lay out for Job the difference in their levels of intelligence. He never calls Job stupid, because he was intelligent. It is just that the level of intelligence God has is so far above our intelligence that it is inconceivable. God gives example after example of His knowledge versus the understanding of Job. God created the universe. He knows what is in it and how it works, while we are still trying to discover it.

God still has intimate knowledge of His creation.

Within that passage in Job, we find that God still has intimate knowledge of the day-to-day workings of His creation. In other words, God's knowledge of this universe did not stop with merely creating it. Nor is His knowledge limited to the past. The universe is always changing, and God is aware of each and every change.

For instance, according to Job, God knows when animals are hungry and provides food for them (Job 38:39-41). He knows when mountain goats give birth, and even when they conceived (39:1-4). He is not a God who is far off, and has no knowledge of what is going on in this world. He is not sitting around out in the cosmos somewhere doing His own thing, completely unconcerned about this earth and its inhabitants. His eye is right here.

We looked at God's omnipresence in the last chapter. And, as we said, the omniscience, or all knowingness, of God is partly a result of His omnipresence. He is right there to see everything that happens. Nothing gets by Him. Therefore, He knows everything that goes on in this universe, even here on earth.

God causes each plant to grow. Psalm 104:14, says that God causes the grass to grow for the cattle, and other plants for man to eat. He knows when animals and people are hungry. He is aware of each plant as it grows, and keeps watch on it. Unfortunately, there are people like me in the world who tend to kill any plant they touch. God knows when they die as well.

Jesus uses the creative imagination of God as an illustration during one of His sermons. It is recorded in Matthew 6:28-30. Jesus tells how God "clothes" the flowers. He makes each and every flower beautiful. In the town where I live there is a huge garden. Tourists even come to see it. As you walk through you see hundreds of different kinds of flowers and plants. Every single one was designed by the mind of God, and they are all beautiful.

But God not only knows what is going on with plants, He knows what is going on with animals as well. We have already mentioned the passage in Job which talks about the animals. Now let us look at what Jesus had to say. Just prior to His comment about the plants, Jesus makes a comment about birds (Matthew 6:26). Jesus says that God, with His knowledge, knows the birds are hungry, and directs them where to find food.

Jesus mentions birds a second time when He declares that God knows when a single bird dies (Matthew 10:29). Even we consider that insignificant. But God places enough importance to that event to know about it. Think about all the birds that die on the grill of a car. God knows about each and every one of them.

Following up the statement about birds, Jesus says that God even knows how many hairs each person has on their head (Matthew 10:30). For some it would be easy for Him to count, but others could prove more of a challenge. Think about it. God knows you so well that He knows how many hairs you have on your head. That is getting very personal.

But God does not stop with simply knowing what is on our head; He knows what is in our head. Psalm 139:1-4 tells us that God knows all of our thoughts. He knows what we are going to do before we do it. Before we ever form the words, God knows what we are going to say. God knows everything that we are thinking. That is intimate knowledge. God knows more about us than we know about ourselves.

We should never believe for a second that God does not know what is going on in this universe. He did not create it and then forget about it. He is actively involved in knowing everything that happens at all times. Because of this, he is personally aware and concerned for each individual on this planet.

God knows possibilities.

God not only knows what is going on physically in the here-and-now, but He also knows what all the possibilities are for the future. Isaiah 48:17-19 tells us that God knows what the possibilities are if other choices are made. In other words, God knows what would have happened if we had run that red light instead of stopping. In the Isaiah passage God is telling the people what would have happened if they had simply obeyed His directions. But, they did not follow His lead and they ended up in bad circumstances.

Jesus alludes to this ability of God to know the possibilities when he scolds certain cities for not believing Him, even though He was preaching and doing miracles within these cities (Matthew 11:20-24). If these other cities Jesus mentions, Tyre, Sidon, and Sodom, had seen miracles like the ones those people witnessed, they would have turned to God. Instead, these cities were destroyed.

With every action, with every decision, there is a myriad of possibilities. We can think of it like a tree. The trunk moves skyward until there is a split. A decision has to be made where to go. If you follow one path, it leads you to one group of branches with each fork being a possibility. If you follow the other path, there are other branches with different possibilities. Where you end up depends on the choices you make.

God knows what each branch is on the tree long before we make our first decision. He can see where each path leads us. It is hard for me to imagine that God knows all of the possibilities in my life. And yet, He not only knows the possibilities of my life; He knows the possibilities of ever person's life. He knows where each decision will lead, and the consequence of every action.

God knows the choices we make.

God not only knows what the possibilities are for our life, He knows which choices we will make. An example of this is found in Exodus 3:19. God is speaking to Moses about leading the people of Israel out of Egypt. He tells Moses that Pharaoh will not allow the people to leave. God knew the choice Pharaoh was going to make.

How does God know what choice we are going to make? Remember that we said God was omnipresent not only physically, but also in time? God is also eternal, existing in all time at the same time. So, God sees what decisions are made as we make them, while at the same time, He knows what they will be before we make them. In other words, God is seeing us in our present and future at the same time. He knows what decision we will make.

Some people get confused on this point and believe that God makes us decide a certain way. In fact, they point to this passage in Exodus, and some of the other passages that give us the full story of the Exodus from Egypt, to show that God forced Pharaoh to not let the people go. This is not true. God has given us free will, and He allows us to exercise it.

Let me try to explain this by using the example of Pharaoh. God said that Pharaoh will not let the people leave Egypt. In other passages it says that God hardened Pharaoh's heart. In other words, God would not let Pharaoh change his mind about the decision to keep the people there. So, did God make the decision for Pharaoh? No.

God saw the future at the same time that He was talking to Moses. He knew what the reaction of Pharaoh would be; that He would not let the people leave. So God forewarned Moses that this was going to happen. After Pharaoh had made his choice, then God would not let him change his mind until God proved to Pharaoh and the rest of the Egyptians exactly who they were dealing with. Pharaoh had the free will to let the people leave the first time Moses asked, but he chose to not let them leave.

At no time will God force us to do anything. He will lay out for us what the consequences of our choices are going to be, and He will allow us to suffer those consequences. But, He will never make the choice for us. Of course, it is always better to listen to God because He does know what the consequences are going to be.

> God knows how everything is put together, and how it runs, including us. He is active in His knowledge of events of the current time. All of the possibilities are laid before Him even though He knows which choice we will ultimately make.

The Son

As we saw when we discussed Jesus being pre-existent, He was involved in creation. As such, Jesus also understands intimately how things are put together, and how they work.

When Jesus walked this earth, he took on human form. He was fully human, and yet God. Because Jesus was God, He had the characteristic of omniscience, even while walking this earth in human form. The human part of Jesus could never have had this ability, but, because He was completely submissive to His spirit side, which is the God part, He was able to have this ability.

Let me give you some examples. In the last chapter we discussed how Jesus saw Nathaniel under the tree, even though it was a great distance from Him (John 1:43-50). Our focus in the last chapter was omnipresence, but Jesus also exhibited omniscience during this encounter with Nathaniel.

Jesus had never met Nathaniel, yet He knew his deepest character trait. He knew Nathaniel was a very honest person who spoke what he thought (John 1:47, 48). Nathaniel was amazed that Jesus knew this about him. As well he should have been. It takes time to know someone's character, and Jesus knew Nathaniel's strongest point without ever having met him before. This could only come from Jesus having an omniscient knowledge of Nathaniel. Along with Jesus declaring He had seen Nathaniel under the tree, Jesus knowing Nathaniel's character was enough to convince him that Jesus was the Son of God.

Jesus always seemed to know what people were thinking, especially the religious leaders who opposed Him. I'll just share two examples with you. In the book of Mark 2:6-8, we see Jesus healing a paralyzed man who has been brought to Jesus by his friends. Jesus makes a controversial statement. He declares that He is forgiving the man's sin. The religious leaders in the house begin thinking to themselves, "Who does this guy think he is? No one can forgive sin except God." Jesus knows what they are thinking and answers their question before they even have time to voice their objection. This account is also found in Matthew 9:1-7.

Another time, Jesus is attending a synagogue on the Sabbath and He sees a man with a withered hand. The religious leaders are very quiet and do not say a word. Jesus knows what they are thinking. "It is wrong to do work on the Sabbath. If this man heals someone on the Sabbath that is work, he will be defying God's law and we can expose him for a fraud." Once again, Jesus answers their thoughts before they are even spoken. Knowing their thoughts, Jesus leaves as the religious leaders begin to plot against Him (Mark 3:1-7).

Jesus had some friends named Lazarus, Martha and Mary. They were brother and sisters who lived in Bethany, and were a favorite visiting place for Jesus. One day, Jesus received word that Lazarus was sick. Jesus knew that Lazarus was very ill, but He stayed where He was for two more days. He finally tells His disciples that Lazarus is dead, even though He had no natural way of knowing this. As they arrive in Bethany, Jesus and His followers are told that Lazarus has been dead for four days. Jesus knew what was going on with His friends, even though He was miles away from them (John 11:1-17).

The Gospel of Luke 19:41-44 records Jesus' approach into Jerusalem the final week of His life. As Jesus rounds a curve on the road to Jerusalem from the Mount of Olives, He spots Jerusalem shining in all its splendor. He begins to weep. As He cries, He pronounces what is going to happen to Jerusalem in the near future. Had the people accepted Him for who He was, God in the flesh, things might have been different. Jesus sees Jerusalem approximately 37 years in the future. He sees the siege ramps against it as the Romans take the city and destroy it. This did occur in 70 AD, 37 years after Jesus walked the earth. His omniscience knew what was coming.

Jesus gives a vivid description of what the future holds for the Jewish nation, and even the world in Matthew chapters 24 and 25. He tells it as if He is watching it take place and just giving a news report about the events surrounding Him. But, many of the things Jesus mentions have not happened yet.

Jesus was always aware of His impending death by crucifixion. As early as John 3, when Jesus is speaking with a religious leader named Nicodemus, we see Jesus making reference to His death (John 3:14-15). He tells the disciples directly of His coming crucifixion several times. One example is found in Matthew 20:17-19. Contrary to what some people want to believe, Jesus was not surprised by the authorities and drug off to be crucified. Nor, did He miscalculate the reaction of the Jewish and Roman officials and end up dead. He knew all along how things were going to play out.

Jesus even knew who was going to betray Him, and who would deny Him. We are told that during the final Passover meal, on the night He was betrayed, Jesus identified Judas as His betrayer, and even let him leave to accomplish his mission (John 13:21-30). Then He told Peter that he would deny knowing Jesus three times before dawn (John 13:38). Peter does deny knowing Jesus three times as he is in the courtyard of the High Priest's house awaiting news of the trial of Jesus (Luke 22:54-62).

It is evident from the accounts of the life of Jesus that He did not lay aside His omniscience while He was in human form on earth. Jesus was still fully God and exercising His abilities as Deity.

The Holy Spirit

The Holy Spirit was also involved in creating the world, and therefore knows how everything is put together, and how it works. But, does His knowledge extend beyond that?

God asks this question of people through the prophet Isaiah: "Who instructed, or taught the Spirit of God so that He would have knowledge (Isaiah 40:13-14)?" The answer, of course, is no one did. The Holy Spirit already knew everything.

The Apostle Paul tells us that the Holy Spirit searches our heart to know what we need to pray to God (Romans 8:26-27). Sometimes we do not know what is really bothering us. We just know that something is not right, and we do not feel good about something. The Holy Spirit knows exactly what is wrong, and helps us to pray appropriately to God about it. If we don't know the words to express it, the Holy Spirit launches His own prayer for us. So, the Spirit knows the hearts of people, their inmost thoughts, even better than the person does.

The Holy Spirit also knows the deep things of God (1 Corinthians 2:10-11). He knows everything God knows, as He should since He is God. This is a clear statement that the Holy Spirit is omniscient.

No one had to teach the Holy Spirit anything for Him to know it. It was already known. The Holy Spirit knows the thoughts and deepest needs of people even better than they do. And God knows everything God knows. I do not know how anyone could be more omniscient than that.

> *God is the only being you can call a know-it-all and it would be true, not an insult.*

Brush Strokes

David says in Psalm 139:13 that God wove him, or knit him, in his mother's womb. In other words, God had a plan and a design for David in creating him. David's body and life were unique, even in the womb. He was not just some accident of nature, He was planned by the God who made the universe.

Each of us can say what David claimed. We have been carefully planned and designed by God. We are not some cosmic accident of protoplasm coming together. There is purpose behind our existence. God, with His omniscience, blueprinted and built us according to unique specifications.

We now know a lot more than David did about how intricate the design of each human is. Since the discovery of DNA we are now able to se that each person has a unique set of DNA. No two people can have exactly the same DNA. This is why it is allowable as evidence in court, just like fingerprints, only better.

From the moment of conception, when the sperm penetrates the egg and forms a single cell, the person's DNA is set. It is unique from the DNA of the father or the mother, although it carries some of each parent's characteristics. With its own DNA in place this cell is technically no longer a part of the mother, it is its own being. Were this cell still a part of the mother's body, such as the liver or appendix, it would still have the same DNA as the mother. But, it does not. It is different and separate from any other part of the mother's body.

Once the DNA is in place, the blueprint for this being is completely mapped out. The DNA makes this cell alive. Inanimate objects, such as rocks and dirt, do not have DNA. Only living things such as plants, animals and humans, have DNA. The blueprint will only allow this cell to be human. It cannot be plant or animal, it is human. So, as it grows, it will always remain human.

From the moment of conception this cell is human. As it divides and grows, we eventually see the shape of what we would consider a baby. But, whether it is in the form of a baby that we recognize, or just a single cell, it is human. God has designed this child, this person, with His infinite wisdom and knowledge. Can you imagine packing all the information needed to form you as an adult into a miniscule part of a cell that you cannot even see?

From what science tells us, the DNA and genes of our body are still running through their blueprint, up until the time we die. They determine our physical characteristics, as well as our susceptibility to certain diseases. That little bit of DNA from that single cell is never finished working out its plan. Only a God of infinite knowledge could create something like that.

What is great about this is that each and every person is unique and specially made. This is no assembly line manufacturing. God planned each and every person. Even identical twins do not have the same exact DNA, making them unique from each other. It is awesome when you consider the thought God put into each and every one of us. Never let anyone tell you that you are not special.

God Almighty

By merely speaking, God was able to create the universe (Genesis 1:1-3). He did not recite some incantation to a power higher than Himself. It was by the force of His own will that the universe came into existence. As God spoke, things were created: light, sun, moon, stars, plants and animals. The power of God is unlimited. He is omnipotent (omni = all, potent = power). The word used 59 times in the Bible to describe God is Almighty.

Omnipotence is a characteristic that can only exist in one being in the universe. Many beings could be spirit, and others could be composed of a trinity. More than one being could be eternal, or know everything. And, two or more beings could possibly be present everywhere at once. However, when it comes to omnipotence, there can only be one being to hold that title. For two beings with equal strength would mean that they could not be more powerful than the other, and therefore, neither one is all powerful.

The other characteristics of God make Him different and unique from His creation. But, maybe we think that there are other beings out there like God. Almost every culture has had gods it worshipped, but only one God is distinct with being all powerful. Only one God could possibly be all powerful. The gods of the other cultures usually controlled only one aspect of nature, such as the sun, the weather, or fertility. God controls everything with His power. There is no limitation to His influence.

God the Father

God reveals Himself as almighty for the first time to a man called Abram (Genesis 17:1). It was important that God revealed this aspect of His being to this man at this time. God was about to make an impossible promise to Abram. It was a promise that only an all powerful being could have kept.

Abram was ninety-nine years old, and his wife Sarai was ninety, when God came to him and promised him a country of his own, that he could hand down to his heirs. God even changed the names to Abraham and Sarah to show how serious He was. Abraham means father of a great multitude, and Sarah means princess. This is all very astonishing when you consider the fact that these two did not have any children.

Abraham's first reaction to God's promise was to laugh (Genesis 17:17). It was also Sarah's first reaction (Genesis 18:12). I imagine that would have been mine too. But, that is why God revealed Himself as all powerful. Only an all powerful being could have been able to get a ninety year old woman to give birth to a son. That child was healthy, and grew up to have children of his own. Abraham's grandchild was Jacob, also known as Israel. Israel had twelve sons, which became the patriarchs of the twelve tribes of Israel. All those of Jewish descent in the world today came from Isaac, Abraham's son. God has certainly displayed His power in keeping His promise to Abraham to provide descendants.

For over four hundred years the descendants of Abraham were enslaved in Egypt. At that time, Egypt was the world power. It was the most advanced technologically and militarily. Pharaoh was considered god, along with the other gods they worshipped. It would take an all powerful being to rescue the people of Israel out of the hands of the Egyptians.

God appeared to Moses and told him that his ancestors knew Him as the Almighty God. He would be the one powerful enough to free the people from Egyptian bondage. God launched ten plagues against the Egyptians in order to prove He was more powerful than their gods. The last plague even struck the house of Pharaoh, killing the heir to the throne. Pharaoh was no god, and definitely not a match for the Almighty (Exodus 6-12).

Later, God revealed Himself as one who does not get tired, or diminish in power (Isaiah 40:28). God's power never diminishes, never slackens. There is never any weakness in Him. He can speak the universe into existence, and still maintain the same power. We constantly have to replenish our energy with food and sleep. God does not have to refill His supply of energy or power.

The Apostle Paul uses passages from various Old Testament scriptures to try to keep the members of the Corinthian church from falling back into the idol worship they had just left (2 Corinthians 6:16-18). He concludes by telling the people that the Almighty God has said this.

The Son

Jesus was constantly displaying His power while here on earth. He performed many miracles of healing, control over demons and weather. He even raised the dead.

Matthew 8 gives us a good sampling of the miracles Jesus performed. We see that Jesus has power over sicknesses from verses 1-17. He healed a leper (1-4), a sick servant (5-13), Peter's mother in law of a fever (14-15), and many other people who were sick (16-17). Some of these healings were done with Jesus touching the person, but some were done from a distance.

Jesus also showed His power and control over the spiritual beings called demons. He was able to cast these spirits out with merely a word (16). And, it was not just individual demons He was able to overpower. He was able to cast out a large number at one time (28-34).

The weather is sometimes troublesome to us, but not to Jesus. As He and the disciples travel by boat across the Sea of Galilee, a severe storm blows in. This must have been some storm because it had seasoned fisherman scared they were going to die. But, Jesus simply tells the wind and waves to calm down and the storm is gone (23-27).

I wonder if the words of Psalm 107:25-29 ran through the minds of the disciples at that time. The Psalmist describes seamen in the midst of a fierce storm calling out to God to save them. God calms the storm and they make it safely to shore.

At one point, Jesus had a long teaching session to over 5,000 people. The hour got late, and Jesus told the disciples to provide food for the crowd. They did not have any food. However, one of the disciples, Andrew, found a boy who had five small loaves of bread and two fish. This was enough for the boy's lunch, and maybe supper, but definitely not enough for over 5,000 people to eat.

Jesus took the bread and fish, blessed it, and had the disciples pass it out to the people. Everyone was fed and full. To make sure that the disciples did not think that the people had just decided not to eat, He had them gather up the leftovers. They filled twelve baskets full of the bread that was left over. Jesus had performed a miracle with great power (John 6:1-13).

Some of the people who witnessed this miracle related it to the time when God provided food for Israel in the desert after they had left Egypt (Exodus 16). They confronted Jesus wanting Him to continually feed them, but Jesus refused and pointed them to the spiritual truth that He was the bread of life (John 6:25-66). This caused a contention within the ranks of Jesus' disciples. Many of those who followed Him left that day. They wanted to be taken care of physically instead of spiritually.

Death is something that mankind just cannot conquer. But for an omnipotent God the Son, it is no problem. As Jesus enters a town called Nain, He runs into a funeral procession for a widow's only son. Jesus feels compassion for this woman and raises her son back to life (Luke 7:11-15).

Later on Jesus is in another town when a man named Jairus, who was a leader in the synagogue, came to Jesus about his sick daughter. By the time Jesus arrives, the child is dead and the mourners are in full volume, crying for the child. Jesus takes three of His disciples, and the parents, into the room where the child is lying and raises her back to life (Luke 8:41,42,49-56).

With the last two cases, Jesus was on the scene soon after the death of the person. But, when we come to the story of Lazarus in John 11, we see that Jesus does not arrive until four days after Lazarus has been entombed. Yet, Jesus was still able to raise Lazarus from the dead.

Jesus has great power, but is He really omnipotent? Jesus makes a statement concerning this in John 5:17-21. Jesus is confronting the religious leaders. He has declared that He has the power to forgive sin, something only God could do. Then, He tells them that He has the same power as God the Father. Whatever God the Father does, the Son does. They are equal in power.

The greatest declarations of Jesus being omnipotent are found in the book of Revelation. The context of the passage suggests Jesus is the one speaking to the Apostle John (Revelation 1:8). Jesus says that He is the Almighty, which is the same word used for God to describe His omnipotence.

Later on in Revelation 19:6, we see the occupants of heaven declaring that Jesus now rules the earth, and that He is the omnipotent Lord God. Once again, it is the context that shows us that the people are speaking about Jesus and not God the Father.

The Holy Spirit

There is really not much said in the Bible about the power of the Holy Spirit. And, honestly, there is no direct statement declaring Him to be omnipotent. However, we have already seen that the Holy Spirit has all of the other characteristics of God. And we know that He was instrumental in creation, which takes great power. The circumstantial evidence would more than suggest that the Holy Spirit is all powerful.

The Apostle Paul attributes the miracles performed through him to the Holy Spirit (Romans 15:13-19). These are some of the same miracle Jesus performed while here on earth. The Holy Spirit is powerful, and is God. Paul does not come right out and say it, but he must have believed in the omnipotence of the Holy Spirit.

Discussion of Omnipotence

God poses the question in Genesis 18:14, "Is anything too hard for the Lord?" The answer of course is no. God has unlimited power and ability. He can do anything He wants, when He wants, and how He wants. There is absolutely nothing God cannot do. Let us not get into the silly stuff of, "can God make a rock He cannot pick up?" Why would God want to?

Now, obviously there are some things God could not do physically, like ceasing to be omnipresent, or even omniscient. But, this is not due to a lack of power, it is a matter of being consistent with who He is and not denying His own characteristics. We cannot cease being human and God cannot stop being God.

There is a certain fear attached to this characteristic of God. Since God is powerful enough to do anything He wants, what is stopping Him from being cruel? We see men who have gained power and then used that power to hurt other people. We all know the expression power corrupts, and absolute power corrupts absolutely. Could God's power be corrupted and hurt us unintentionally, or even intentionally, for no reason?

An atomic reaction can produce a huge destructive explosion, or it could produce beneficial energy. The atomic bomb is power out of control, while the nuclear power plant is power under control. God's power is always under control.

Nowhere in the Bible do we find God's power randomly laying waste to anything. The closest we come to an atomic explosion of God's power is when God floods the earth during the time of Noah (Genesis 6-8). But, God was still under control then. He did not destroy everyone and everything. He kept a representation of every species, including humans, alive to repopulate the earth.

God is always specific and deliberate in His use of power. There was a plan with creation, not just a random throwing things into existence and letting them land wherever. With more accuracy than the smart bombs of today, God could pinpoint destruction to punish the ones who were guilty, and still not hurt the innocent. Numbers 16 tells the story of some workers in the tabernacle who rebelled against Moses and Aaron, the High Priest. 250 men conspired to take over the temple, but God destroyed them. He made the earth open and consume everything two of the men had, including their families. Then he sent fire to destroy the rest of the men. God was specific in His use of power.

God does not arbitrarily go off and use His power without a design behind it. Jesus did not arbitrarily use His power either. When Jesus went into the wilderness before starting His public ministry, He stayed there for forty days. He did not eat during that time, so I am sure He was very hungry. Then the devil came to Him and tempted Him. He wanted Jesus to turn some stones into bread. Jesus could have done that without thinking. He was hungry. It would seem logical to feed His body before He died of starvation. But, Jesus did not do it. The stones remained rocks, and Jesus had no bread (Matthew 4:1-4).

It would not have been wrong for Jesus to make food for Himself. But, He would not allow someone else to control Him. The power of God is always under the control of God, not anyone else. Jesus decided that Satan was not going to be the one calling the shots when it came to what miracles were to be done. Jesus showed restraint, and gave us a glimpse of the way God controls His power.

The controlling mechanism of God's power is His moral character, which we will look at in the next section of this study. For now, suffice it to say that God is good, and will not use His power for anything that is evil. I know; all kinds of questions are rising up in your mind right now about God and evil. "Why doesn't God just destroy evil? Why does God allow children to die?" Those questions will be tackled when we discuss God's moral characteristics. This section is only dealing with His physical characteristics.

Some people point out that there are some things God cannot do. According to the Bible God cannot lie (Numbers 23:19; Titus 1:2; Hebrews 6:18). God cannot be tempted to sin (James 1:13). And God cannot deny that He exists (2 Timothy 2:13). But these restrictions are merely examples of God's power being under control. These are limitations imposed by His will in order to uphold His moral character. All of these limitations are moral in nature, not due to a lack of ability or power. If God were to deny He exists, or deny His true nature, then He would be a liar and not a moral being. It takes power under great control to continuously uphold the moral right, and not allow the wrong to enter.

We do not have to be afraid of God's power. Yes, He could wipe us out of existence without even thinking about it. But His moral character will not allow Him to do such a thing. He does not want to use His power maliciously. He wants to use it productively, for our betterment.

Brush Strokes

God created us with physical and mental power. Physically we have the strength to move objects. Some people use their strength in the area of sports and entertain people. Others use their strength to perform manual labor, bringing products to people to make their lives easier. There are also those who use their strength to help out the less fortunate, such as volunteering their time and strength to serve at a food kitchen or some other charity.

Mentally we have figured out ways to make our lives better and easier, as well as ways to save our strength. Instead of trying to move a large amount of items with a bunch of people, we use a forklift. Farming has become more efficient to produce more food, and we have figured out better ways to ship it to where it is needed. Medicines and vaccines have been developed to fight disease. Electricity has been harnessed to run modern conveniences.

We have also developed economic power. Money is used to buy goods. Some of the goods are necessities, like food, and some are luxuries like DVDs. And many people use their economic power to help others through their support of charities and individuals. Some are able to fund research that leads to other discoveries that helps make our lives easier.

The final area of power which has developed is political power. Public service is a high calling. Some people are interested in being leaders in their community or nation in order to effect change that will help the citizens.

All of these powers are good, if they are kept under control. When physical power gets out of control it becomes battery and abuse. Mental loss of control will see us developing weapons of mass destruction to be used offensively against others, instead of nuclear power plants to help people live more comfortably. It develops toxins to kill instead of medicines to heal. Greed is the byproduct of economic power out of control. It will gather more to itself even if it hurts other people. Finally, dictatorship and misuse of the office are the results of political power out of control.

It is when we stop looking at how we can use our power to help others that we get into trouble. The more self-centered our use of power becomes, the more out of control it gets. God is never egocentric about the use of His power. He always does what is best for others, even if we don't see it. We need to follow God's example by keeping our power under control.

Section Summary

We have made it through the first part of our study. The physical characteristics of God have come alive before our eyes as we have looked at the lines and markings God has used to reveal His portrait to us in the Bible. Perhaps the thing that stands out most about this section is that God is not anything like us. In fact, it is hard for us to grasp a reference point from which to gain an accurate picture of Him.

In the first chapter we found out that God is a spirit being, without shape, or form, or boundary. He is not composed of flesh and blood as we are. This essence, or substance, which is God's physical form, allows Him to have physical characteristics that are unmatched, and unknown, in this universe.

One of these characteristics, and probably the most confusing, is that God is a trinity. God is a single entity, but at the same time He is three beings. The Father, Son, and Holy Spirit are all three God collectively and individually. While they are all the same entity, each being has His own personality and mission. The three are one, and the one is three. The essence, or central part, of each being of the trinity is spirit.

Because God is spirit, He is an eternal being. There has never been a time when God did not exist, and there will never be a time when He ceases to exist. We saw that this was true for the Father, Son, and Holy Spirit. All three are self-existent, not having to rely on anyone or anything to exist or to continue existing.

God is immense, which allows Him to be physically present everywhere. All three members of the entity of God are also omnipresent. God has no physical boundaries, so He can be physically and consciously present everywhere all at one time. Time is not a boundary to God as He can be in the past, present and future all at once. Even Jesus, the Son, was omnipresent while He was walking this earth in human form.

Working hand-in-hand with omnipresence is omniscience. Because God is everywhere at once, He knows everything that is happening. But God knows much more than just the facts of events. He knows what we are thinking and intending to do. He knows all of the options we have, and all of the possibilities of consequences to actions we might take. He also knows which decisions we will make. We found that Jesus also displayed this quality while here on earth.

Finally, we learned that God is almighty, or omnipotent. There is absolutely nothing God cannot do. However, He does choose not to do certain things that might compromise His moral integrity. God's power is always under control. The miracles of Jesus exhibited some of God's power on earth.

Physical characteristics are highly impersonal. We cannot tell the character of a person by just looking at their physical features. When many artists paint, they end up with a person that may have just as well been a bowl of fruit. There is no life, no personality given to the subject of the portrait. But, the great artists are able to paint subtle expressions on the face, or a certain look in the eye, to express a subject's mood or character. It is the difference between looking at the stick figure drawing of a child and the Mona Lisa. With only the physical characteristics of God we have nothing more than the outline of a drawing. But, God is a master painter. In the next section we will see Him begin to fill in the colors as He expresses His inner, moral, character.

FILLING IN THE COLORS

THE MORAL CHARACTERISTICS OF GOD

✦

HOLY
JUST
LOVE
MERCY
TRUE

God Is Holy

Holy may be an unfamiliar word to you. Outside of the occasional "Holy lunch-meat Batman," or "She has a holier than thou attitude," you may not have heard the word much. What does it mean? The word is often used in a church setting, but it is doubtful very many of the faithful church goers have a strong concept of what this word entails. And yet, it appears that, if holy was a color, it would be the most used color by God to paint His portrait.

Building A Definition Of Holiness

So, what is being holy, or holiness? We must look at how the Old Testament writers viewed, or used, the word holy. This is important because the New Testament writers gained their concept of the meaning of the word holy from the Old Testament. In the Old Testament we see that the word holy is used to describe objects, people, and God. As we look at the multitude of passages containing the word holy, we see that the common theme is separation.

For instance, in Leviticus 22 God lays down the rules for how the priests are supposed to treat the objects in the temple that are considered holy. He lists times when they are to remain separated from the holy things. If a priest was defiled, or dirty, morally, physically in regard to health, or just physically dirty, he was not to approach the things considered holy. There was to be no contamination on those special objects.

According to the Ten Commandments, we are to keep the Sabbath day holy (Exodus 20:8). It was to be separate and different than all the other days. It was to be set aside as special. The Sabbath was not holy just because people worshipped God on that day. It was holy because it was different than all the other days. This was the day that God commanded people to sit down and relax from all the work they had done the rest of the week. And it was the one day they were to spend their time thinking about God and worshipping Him instead of focusing on their work.

Israel as a nation was to be holy (Exodus 19:5,6). They were to be separate and different than the other nations of the world. They would be the ones who worshipped the true God, and Him alone. Israel was unique in that they worshipped only one God, while everyone else worshipped multiple Gods.

This idea of separation becomes clearer when we look at Numbers chapter 6. Within this chapter are the rules that a person taking the vow of a Nazarite must follow. The Nazaritic vow was an oath to serve God, and to worship Him for a certain time period. The word separate appears many times in this passage, and is connected to the word holy. God says this man will be separate, and this man will be considered holy. He is separated from the common people to do a special service, or time of worship, to God.

The Old Testament writers seemed to use the word holy in the context of being set apart, to be quarantined from everything else. Basically speaking it could mean being pure, unblemished by anything that is dirty or spotted, morally or physically. It is remaining protected from contamination.

But, there is also the sense in the Old Testament where being holy means that there is a clear distinction between right and wrong. The person who is holy is the one who consistently does what is right instead of what is wrong. Two examples we have seen are the Nazarite and the priests. For God this is taken a step further. God always does what is right. He never does what is wrong.

If we combine the ideas of being separate and being good, I believe the word holy, or to be holy, could be defined as embracing what is right, to the exclusion of what is wrong. In other words, a person who is holy is so busy doing what is considered right and good, that they do not have time to do wrong, or bad.

This definition would also fit for objects. The Bible often mentions that objects are holy, especially those used in the temple to worship God. This means that the object is to be used solely for good, or for doing what is right (like worshipping God), instead of anything that is bad, or wrong. The Sabbath would be a day set a side for doing what is right. So the concept of being set aside fits in with this part of the definition as well. An object is set aside to do good, and then protected from being contaminated or being used in a wrong way.

Holiness—Embracing what is right to the exclusion of what is wrong.

God and Holiness

How does God determine what is right and wrong?

God would have to know the difference between right and wrong in order to be holy. Does God have a set of rules to follow? No. If God had to follow a set of rules, then the rules would be greater than God. They would command Him and determine His actions. But God determines His own actions. Remember, God is self-existent and therefore free of anything that might restrain Him, even rules.

If He does not have rules to follow, then what does God use as a guide to judge right from wrong? As far as I can tell God's holiness, always embracing what is right to the exclusion of what is wrong, is completely dependent on God's omniscience. Remember that God knows everything, including all possibilities of the outcome of an action. If we define wrong as anything that creates a negative consequence against a person, then we can easily see how God is always able to do the right thing. Because God can see all possibilities, He simply looks at an action, or thought, and knows if it will ultimately have a positive or negative consequence. All actions which could have a negative consequence are deemed wrong, and God does not do them.

Let me try to give a couple of examples. God says that murder is wrong. I believe that is obvious, even to us. Murder has drastic negative consequences for the victim and the perpetrator. Telling lies about someone is also deemed wrong by God. Not only does it hurt the person lied about, but the person who lied must now work to keep his story straight, which causes unnecessary stress. These are negative consequences. I have never met anyone who committed adultery who said that there were no negative consequences to the affair.

There are just some things that are going to produce negative results no matter who does the action, or when it is done. God gave us some examples with the Ten Commandments (three of which I just listed in the previous paragraph). Then there are those things which, in our eyes, are gray areas. Sometimes they may seem right, but at other times they are wrong. God, because of His omniscience, never has that problem. There is never a gray area with God, only black and white. He knows what the consequences are for every action or thought. He always knows what is right.

God always does what is right. This is not a conscious decision by Him. Instead it is a part of His being. It is more a matter of the heart than the will. If He were human we would say that it is a part of His DNA. It is just not within

God to do anything that would cause a detrimental consequence to Himself or to someone else. In this sense, God is the source of holiness.

Can God be around evil?

So, we have determined that being holy means embracing what is right to the exclusion of what is wrong. So, what about this matter of separation that is so prominent in the Bible contexts concerning holiness? Does this mean that God cannot be around anyone who has done something wrong? Does God quarantine Himself from anything that is evil, or bad?

Satan is the most evil being we know of, and yet God had at least two meetings with him (Job 1:6-12; 2:1-7). The book of Revelation shows us that Satan and his angelic followers are in heaven before they are cast out (Revelation 12:7-9). Even Satan has access to God. That does not sound like God has established a no evil boundary around Him.

If it were true that God could have no contact with anything that is bad, or any person who does wrong, then the Holy Spirit would never be able to live within imperfect people. Christians are forgiven, but they are not perfect. Jesus says in John 16:7-11, that the Holy Spirit will convince the people of the world about sin. This means that the Holy Spirit would have to interact with people who are evil, and who have never accepted Jesus as the payment for their sin. In other words, in order to convince people of their need for God in their life, the Holy Spirit will have to interact with those who refuse God, and who sin.

It does not appear true that God quarantines Himself from evil. Instead, James 1:13-17 gives us a better picture of God. He cannot be tempted to sin. God is so holy that He repels evil. It has no place in Him, and there is no room for evil to enter. Do you remember the taunt, "I'm rubber, you're glue, whatever you say bounces off me and sticks to you"? God is rubber when it comes to evil. Evil bounces off of Him without leaving a mark. That is what James means when He calls God the Father of Lights.

There is no shadow, no impurity, within God's being. He is pure holiness. Everything we know to be good, or consider as good, comes from God. He is the source of goodness, the source of holiness, within the universe.

This part of the study has really changed the way I think about God. I have always thought of holiness as keeping things away. Follow the rules and keep away from bad things. But, it is actually the reverse. Holiness is not staying away from bad things; it is being filled with good things.

Jesus gives an illustration of this in one of His parables. In Matthew 12:43-45, Jesus speaks about a demon leaving a person. This demon roams around, but soon decides to return to the person. The person is all swept clean and looks nice and neat, and invitingly empty. The demon gets some of his friends to join him at his house inside the person. The picture here is of someone who followed the rules. They did everything right, and they were clean. But, there was nothing there to repel evil. When holiness is involved it not only cleans the house, it fills it up so that evil cannot return.

Holiness is not a matter of the will. God could willfully follow rules and always do what is right. But, then there would still be that empty space where evil could possibly creep in. Instead, holiness is a matter of the heart. It is the very core nature of God to be good, to be holy, which fills Him completely to overflowing. His heart beats goodness. God does not have to build walls, or isolate Himself from evil. Nothing bad can touch God or penetrate His being. He is an absolute purity of goodness and right; completely filled to the point nothing else has room to enter.

I believe it is the misconception that holiness involves staying away from anything evil which has caused us to have the picture of God as a cosmic killjoy. We see God as making rules and regulations to keep us from doing things that look fun. We believe that we have to live our life in monasteries in order to stay away from evil and temptation. But the holiness of God is all about being filled with goodness. It is not about God wanting us to stay away from evil. Instead, it is Him wanting us to experience goodness. God does not want us to experience negative consequences. He wants us to experience all the good consequences. That is not killing our fun; it is giving us an easier, happier life.

What about the wrath of God?

Let us not think that the holiness of God is not against evil, or just excuses it. Like light piercing darkness, holiness pierces evil and defeats it. The holiness of God hates evil because it causes negative consequences. Evil causes pain, suffering, and death. When we read through the Bible we may get the idea that God is angry all the time because people do not obey His rules. But, the truth is, God is angry, and fighting against the evil which causes so many negative consequences for people.

As we read the Old Testament, we see the word wrath and anger a lot in reference to God. This does not mean that God is some cranky old codger who gets mad at the drop of a hat. If you examine the passages closely, you will find that almost every one of them is related to holiness. Whenever God becomes angry, it is because someone is about to disobey Him and cause something to lose its holiness, or separateness. The wrath of God is never an out of control rage like we would think of with a person. It is an exact, surgical strike with power to eliminate the person, or people, who are causing a threat to holiness.

I have come to think of the wrath of God in this way. Holiness and evil are like cold air overriding warm air. Always in motion as one wants to go one direction, while the other desires the opposite. Eventually a funnel cloud will form, spiraling with increasing wind strength. The cloud is fine as long as it stays in the air, but when it touches the ground, it becomes very destructive.

The wrath of God, His holiness exerting itself over evil, is like that tornado. Usually it is just a funnel cloud swirling in conflict beyond our sight, and not causing any damage. But, sometimes, the conflict touches down into the lives of people as evil embeds itself in them. The visible and horrible effects are the destruction of the people as the holiness of God conflicts with the evil within them.

Fortunately, the wrath of God is prevalent only in the Old Testament. The display of anger is not nearly as dramatic when we get to the New Testament, although Ananias and Sapphira might not agree (Acts 5:1-11). They were killed during the period of the early church when they lied to God. Paul seemed to feel that the wrath of God was making people sick, and some die, because they were not keeping the observance of the last supper holy (1 Corinthians 11:20-34). God has done everything He can to curb it, but the conflict between evil and God's holiness still strikes people.

I know we really do not like to think about God in this way. We like to think of God as a God of love, not wrath. But consider this. If a rattlesnake were about to strike at your child, would you yell at the snake and threaten to punish it, or just kill it as fast as you could? Sometimes evil gets to the point where it is a rattlesnake poised to strike innocent people and spread its venom. Out of a holy love God takes swift and decisive action to protect as many people as He can from being bitten. As you read the accounts in the Old Testament of God's wrath on someone, try to think of it like this: God's anger is not destroying someone; His love is keeping others from being poisoned.

Conclusion

We have seen that holiness is not just putting up a wall to keep evil out. That would be a defensive position. Holiness takes an offensive position. It roots out evil to defeat it. The Ten Commandments are really proactive. By identifying the major problem areas where evil invades our lives, God was going on the offensive to protect us from it. But, He also gave us positive things to do, like worship Him on the Sabbath, in order to help us be filled with holiness, which would help repel evil. And sometimes, God steps in to protect us with His wrath.

God the Father

As was stated in the beginning of this chapter, if holiness was a color, it would be the most prominent color in the portrait God is painting. It would also be a primary color, as it is the absolute core of God's being.

In Leviticus 19, God begins giving Israel the moral law they were to follow. And He starts by declaring to Moses that He is holy (Leviticus 19:2). True holiness is needed in order to create a moral law for people to follow. Anyone can follow a law, but only a person who can foresee the negative consequences of an action can develop a moral law. And, only a person who is holy, who has the best interest of everyone in mind, can actually formulate the law into a universal code. God wanted to be sure that the people understood His credentials were in line with the job He was taking on in dishing out a moral code.

God declares His name to be Holy in Isaiah 57:15. God was not saying that His name was sacred. He was declaring that "Holy" actually is His name. Isaiah must have grasped the point because he calls God the Holy One approximately thirty times in his book. In fact, the first time Isaiah sees God, he hears the angels with God declaring that God is "holy, holy, holy" (Isaiah 6:3). The Apostle John had the same experience, and recorded it in Revelation 4:8.

The prophet Habakkuk makes a statement in chapter one verse thirteen of his book which many people misinterpret. He says that God cannot look on evil. Many people interpret this to mean that God must keep Himself separated from evil. We have already seen that other passages of scripture would seem to contradict this interpretation.

In order to understand how to interpret this expression from Habakkuk, we must understand the context. Habakkuk lived in Judah, which was the southern kingdom of Israel after their civil war. Israel had already fallen to Assyria, and God had just told Habakkuk that Babylon was going to defeat Judah and take them into captivity. Israel had been destroyed because they had worshipped other gods, and Judah was now going to fall for the same reason.

What Habakkuk could not understand was how God could use the Babylonians to punish Judah. After all, the Babylonians were worse than Judah when it came to worshipping other gods. They did not even acknowledge that the true God existed.

Habakkuk 1:13 is not an absolute statement on the nature of God. It is a representation of God's character. The author is saying, "God, You have more character than to let these evil people overpower the good people of Judah." Habakkuk's basic question is, "Why is God using these wicked people?" The actions of God just did not seem to mesh with what Habakkuk new about God's character.

The fact that God used the Babylonians to punish Judah proves that God can look on evil people. God can even interact with evil people, as He did with the Babylonians in helping them defeat Judah.

God the Son

Jesus declares that He is Holy in Revelation 3:7. This is the only outright statement by Jesus of His holiness. However, there is an implied statement by Jesus.

We often find Jesus verbally sparring with the Pharisees, the religious leaders of His day. On one such occasion Jesus told them that He always did what pleased God the Father (John 8:28, 29). This means that Jesus never did anything which God would not approve. Since God would never approve of doing anything which had a negative consequence to it, Jesus must have never done any such thing. This means that Jesus never did anything which was wrong.

But, this passage shows more than just following the rules God lays out. Jesus says that He always listened to the Father. He had a close relationship with the Father. Jesus filled His life up with the goodness of God to the point where there was no place for doing anything wrong. That is our definition of holiness.

The Holy Spirit

Every time the Holy Spirit is mentioned it is a declaration of His holiness. The name is statement enough. It is plain and simple, and could not be any clearer.

Brush Strokes

Brush Strokes is going to take on a little different quality as we progress through this section of the characteristics of God. In discussing the physical attributes of God we looked at how they would affect our life. But, with the moral attributes, we are going to see how they are to apply to our life.

Let me explain. There is no way that we could have the physical characteristics of God. We could never be omnipotent or omnipresent. And God would never expect us to have those abilities. But, when we come to the moral characteristics of God, we are commanded to possess them. They are to be a part of our life.

In Leviticus 19:2, God tells the people of Israel that they are supposed to be holy because He is holy. The Apostle Peter states the same idea in his letter, and even quotes the passage from Leviticus to emphasize his point (1 Peter 1:15, 16). I do not believe God would command us to do something that was not possible.

So, what does it mean for us to be holy? Our definition of holiness is the embracing of what is right to the exclusion of what is wrong. Like God, this does not mean that we have to isolate ourselves from everything that is bad. It does mean that, like Jesus, we fill our life up with the goodness of God through a relationship with Him, so that we do not have any room for evil to come into our life.

Does this mean that we have to follow a lot of rules? I believe we saw that rules did not apply to God. Following rules is a matter of the will. Even the most evil person can follow rules if he wants. Holiness is a matter of the heart. It is the inner desire to do what is right. Rules usually define what is wrong, what we should not do. But, holiness does what is right, even when there is not a rule to define it.

Jesus gave us a good example of the difference between rules and holiness. As Jesus was teaching in the temple one day, all of the religious leaders decided to gang up on Him and give Him tests to see if He would trip up with His words so they could arrest Him, or get the people to hate Him. They did not succeed. However, one man came forward with an honest question. He wanted to know which of the many commandments God had given was the greatest. This was a huge debate in the religious circles of the time.

In responding to this man's question, Jesus takes the rules of the Ten Commandments, and turns them into the way of holiness (Matthew 22:35-40). The Ten Commandments showed us what was wrong, what we should and should not do. But Jesus took all those rules and turned them around to the source of holiness. He said that we should love God with all of our being, and our neighbor the same as we love ourselves.

Someone could conceivably follow the Ten Commandments and still not be holy. Like I said, even an evil person can follow rules. Jesus focused on the heart of the person, not the mind. It is from a heart of love for God and others that we are motivated to do what is right and best for them. If we were to always act on that motivation, then the Ten Commandments, or any laws, would not be necessary. This attitude, or motivation, is true holiness.

We are not perfect beings, and we are not omniscient to where we always know the right thing to do. God knows that. He does not expect perfection; that would be unreasonable. But, He does expect holiness. God wants us to have that desire, that heart and attitude, that loves Him and others enough to want to do what is right. If we can achieve that, then we will be holy as God is holy.

God Is Just

Of all the moral characteristics of God, we are probably the most cynical about this one. God is just, or fair. Righteous is the old fashioned term for it. Face it, in the world we live in there are not many fine examples of justice. Those who commit crimes get off on technicalities while the victims continue to suffer. Judges can be bought, and there is abuse of power in police forces and governments. The rich get richer as they fleece the poor.

We can understand that men, and the system of justice they provide, are going to be corrupt. But then we come to other areas in the world where we question fairness or justice. An innocent child dies of a horrible disease, while a murderer lives a long life. The drunk driver walks away without a scratch, while the innocent driver of the other vehicle takes a final ride to the morgue. The nicest, most caring person in town has to battle cancer, while the meanest grump ever born lives a perfectly healthy life right up to the end. The good die young. We do not understand. God is fair?

Defining Justice

I believe we can all agree on the definition of justice. Justice is getting exactly what you deserve. It means that if you do the crime, you do the time. Being just means that the appropriate punishment is given out for the offense. It also means that the right reward is given out for the action which was good. Because of our limitations, humans have a hard time giving out exactly the right amount of punishment and praise. But, the unlimited God should have no problem.

The base for God's justice is His holiness. The holiness of God will only do what is right and good. Therefore, God can never give out a punishment that is not deserved. Remember that the omniscience of God is the foundation of God's holiness. Because God knows everything, He knows exactly how much punishment is deserved for any given evil action.

We need to realize something as we move forward in this study. There is a difference between justice, or being fair, and life. What do I mean by that? Being fair has to do with giving out the right punishment or reward for some action committed. For example, placing someone in jail for a crime, or giving someone a certificate of achievement for completing a class. Justice and fairness have to do with decisions. The person decided to commit the robbery, the judge decided to place them in jail.

But, life is different. Life is not about punishment or reward, it just happens. For example, one person gets cancer while another does not. The person with cancer is not being punished, it is just life. When the meanest grump in town has an extremely healthy life, he is not being rewarded for being mean. It is just life. Some of the situations listed in the earlier paragraphs where I asked if God was fair, really have no bearing on fairness. They are just life. Life does not come under the jurisdiction of justice or fairness. Instead, it is under the authority of sovereignty, which we will get to in a later chapter.

Why Does Sin Equal Death?

In thinking about the fairness of God, I came across two questions. The first comes from the beginning of the Bible. God created everything, and placed Adam and Eve in the Garden of Eden. He only gave them one rule to follow. "Do not eat the fruit from the tree of the knowledge of good and evil. If you eat the fruit, you will die." That is found in Genesis 2:17. In chapter three Adam and Eve ate. But, they did not die instantly. If the fruit were poison, that would be one thing, but it was not. Apparently the dying part God mentioned was a punishment He was going to inflict. So, how fair is that when you get the death penalty for eating a piece of fruit?

That was my first question. The second comes from the book of Romans in the New Testament. The Apostle Paul writes in Romans 6:23 that "the payment for sin is death." My question is simple. Why? Why is the payment for any sin, no matter how small, death? That just does not seem fair. It sounds like God has a messed up sense of justice.

Allow me to work through the answers I came up with for these questions. We need to begin with a definition and explanation of the word sin. It is a term used in church a lot, and found in the Bible. But, what exactly is sin? I have heard sin defined as anything which is against God's will. Another way of saying it would be disobeying God. In a sense this is true, but I do not believe it gives us the full picture of why this is bad. That kind of definition makes me think of a parent telling his child, "Because I said so." It does not answer the child's question of why it should not be done.

As I just said, Genesis chapter three relates the sad story of what is referred to as original sin. Adam and Eve had been created by God and placed in the Garden of Eden. They were perfect, genetically and morally. But then, Satan took on the form of a serpent and tricked Eve into eating the fruit God had told them not to eat. Adam quickly followed suit. Now, why was this particular act so wrong? After all, it was just a piece of fruit.

What was wrong was who Adam and Eve listened to in order to formulate their concept of right and wrong. God is the only omniscient being in the universe. He is the only One who knows what is right and what is wrong all the time. Everyone else will get it wrong, at least occasionally. Eve decided to listen to Satan and make him her source for determining right from wrong. (I don't think I have to explain what a bad idea that was.) Adam then decided to listen to Eve, who had just been deceived, for his source of information about right and wrong.

When we listen to someone other than God, and use them for our source in determining right from wrong, there is going to come a time when we get it wrong. There will come a time when our source just cannot know all of the possibilities, and we will make a decision that has unforeseen negative consequences. However, if we always listen to God, we would never have that problem. God knows all of the possibilities, so there are never unforeseen consequences with Him. Therefore, not listening to God has negative consequences, which is why sin is wrong.

Basically speaking, sin is deciding to follow someone other than God in determining what is right and wrong, and then acting on the advice given. This could even be following our own ideas. God is the only pure source of accurate information when it comes to determining what is right. This is because He is omniscient and holy.

So, what about the death penalty thing? Remember that God is omniscient. He knows the final outcome of every action and choice. When Adam and Eve broke the one rule they had to follow, they started down an unalterable path. They had begun to question whether God really did know what was right and wrong, and that He had their best interest in mind. As God looked forward, He saw that this kind of thinking only led to death.

Adam and Eve would continue to use their own judgment to decide what was right and wrong. Because they could not foresee all of the consequences, they would continue to make wrong choices at times. Eventually their choices would lead to physical death. And, with each choice they made without God they would grow further from Him, causing spiritual death. So, when they ate the fruit, they started down an inevitable path to destruction.

God did place judgment on Adam and Eve for their disobedience. God cursed the earth and brought in weeds and death to plants and animals. Adam was forced to till the ground in order to get food, and Eve was to have pain in childbirth. God also allowed the consequence of their sin to be fully played out. He allowed them to die.

There was another tree in the Garden of Eden. This one Adam and Eve had apparently eaten from before since it was not forbidden. It was called the Tree of Life, and according to the book of Revelation, its leaves have the ability to heal and give life (Revelation 22:2). If humans had the capacity to never die, then the pain and suffering they would cause would have been too much for anyone to bear. God made sure that the consequences of Adam and Eve's actions were carried out all the way to death. That is why they were removed from the garden so they would not eat of the Tree of Life and live forever.

God did not give Adam and Eve a death sentence for eating fruit. He did place a curse on them and make their life harder for disobedience to Him. And, he allowed the consequences of their actions to be fully played out for their sake. If they had not died, they would eventually end up in a constant state of misery as the negative consequences of their choices continued to multiply. God tried to warn them, but they did not listen.

I believe the story of Adam and Eve shows us why even the smallest sin leads to death. It is not the action itself; it is the attitude and thought process behind the action. We decide that God does not know what is right and what is wrong. So, we make the decision ourselves that something is right, and then we do it. If we are wrong it leads to negative consequences, which continue to build throughout our life. The ultimate consequence of not doing what is right is physical death, and separation from the God we would not listen to. Allow me to paraphrase the writer of the Proverbs: Trust God's judgment, not your own, and then you will have a good life (Proverbs 3:5-8).

When we talk of death, we are not necessarily speaking of physical death. That is going to happen. We are talking about the spiritual death we suffer when we are physically separated from God. When we sin, we ultimately end up separated from God because of our actions and attitude. God is just when He pronounces the death sentence for even the smallest infraction. He knows that it is the ultimate end anyway. But, God has done everything He can to keep us from having to face the ultimate consequence of our actions. Jesus died, even though He had never sinned, in order to accept our consequences on Himself. We still deserve to die, that would be the fair thing, but Jesus died instead. We do not have to be permanently separated from God. Because of Jesus, we can live with God for eternity.

God the Father

God declares Himself just in Isaiah 45:21. He is making a comparison between Himself and the false idols of other nations. God is a God of justice. That was almost unheard of in other lands and religions. The gods of the ancient world were generally self-serving. They did not care about justice; they did things according to their own whims and fancies.

If a god was angry, it would strike down anyone, or anything, it wanted. If it was happy, it would give out gifts. Religions grew to appease the god so that good things would happen instead of bad. This is bribery on a divine scale. Pay the god enough and he will be happy with you. That is not justice.

God, on the other hand, is just. Sacrifices were not made to appease God; they were made to pay the price for sin. Animals were sacrificed in order to temporarily take the place of the human in death. Sometimes, God exacts the penalty for sin by killing the people Himself. But, God never strikes someone down, or gives good gifts to someone just on a whim. God cannot be bought or bribed. It does not matter how good, or how bad, a person is. God treats everyone the same.

Moses acknowledged the justice of God (Deuteronomy 32:4). He received the law from God; not just the Ten Commandments, but all the law. Moses viewed the whole system of law and sacrifices that he had received from God and declared that God is just. Moses knew the laws were fair and appropriate. He knew that the sacrifices were to pay the terrible price for sin, not to appease an angry God.

Throughout the forty years of wandering in the wilderness, Moses saw God punish people for their sin and disobedience. Israel was wandering around for forty years because they did not believe that God would give them the land He had promised. All of the people who did not believe God died in the wilderness. Some of them God took out faster than others. One group led a rebellion and God killed them with fire and by burying them in the earth. Some were struck with disease. But in seeing God at work in punishing people, Moses could still say at the end of his life; God is just.

God the Son

Jesus declared His judgment to be just (John 5:30). Because He was in tune with the Father, He was able to do exactly what the Father did. The Father is just, so Jesus was just. Jesus always looked to the Father for answers. Remember what we said about sin and getting our definitions of right and wrong from others? Jesus always got His information from the source.

Three times in the book of Acts, Jesus is identified as being just. The first time is during the Apostle Peter's sermon on the day of Pentecost (Acts 3:14). Stephen, a deacon in the Jerusalem church, gave a speech right before he was stoned to death. In it he called Jesus the Just One (Acts 7:52). Paul used the same words, Just One, to identify Jesus as he was defending himself against a mob in Jerusalem (Acts 22:14). Three different early church leaders identified Jesus as being just. This has apparently been a core value in the church from the beginning.

It is a good thing that Jesus is just because we will all be judged by Him. Christians will come before the judgment seat of Christ (Romans 14:10). They will be given rewards according to their work on earth. And Jesus will judge those who refused to allow God into their life (Revelation 20:11-15). They will be sent to a place where they can live without God forever.

The Holy Spirit

When Jesus told His disciples to expect the coming of the Holy Spirit, He gave them a description of what the Spirit's job would be (John 16:8-14). Part of the Spirit's responsibility is to help people judge between right and wrong. In order to do this accurately, the Holy Spirit must be just. We already know the Spirit is holy, and justice is just an extension, or byproduct of holiness.

Brush Strokes

What does God require from us? We are to live justly (Micah 6:8). Just as God wants us to be holy, He also wants us to be fair. This is stressed several times in the Bible, and touches different areas of our life. The passage in Micah is a call to be just in everything we do, and in our dealings with everyone.

But God also specified being just and fair in our workplace. He did not just mention it once, He mentioned it three times: Leviticus 19:35,36; Deuteronomy 25:15; Ezekiel 45:10. In these passages God is talking about giving a fair measure of food for the proper price. The butcher was not to put his thumb on the scale, and the person selling grain was not to use a smaller scoop. If a person was paying for five pounds of grain, they should receive five pounds of grain.

This has implications for us as well. If we are a manufacturer, we are to produce and deliver a good product. We are not to cut corners. If we are a salesman, then the product better deliver what we promise. If it does not, then we should make it right.

An example came to mind of the differences between a builder working justly, and one who is not fair in his business dealings. When hurricane Andrew, a category five hurricane, hit the Florida coast, it destroyed a lot of houses and buildings. Upon closer inspection it was discovered that some of these buildings should not have sustained damage. These buildings had not been built according to code. The builder had cut corners, and the house was destroyed.

The flip side of that story is a house which is over one hundred years old, and has outlasted numerous hurricanes. Even a category four did not phase it after one hundred years. Personally, I think every house built in an area where there are hurricanes should have to be built to those specifications. That builder obviously did not cut corners.

So, which builder would you want working for you? Then that is the type of person you should be in business. Be honest and just in your dealings with people. Give them the fullest amount, the best product, and the best service.

This really goes beyond products. It also involves being a good worker and employee. The business you work for deserves your best effort. That is only fair. They pay you to work eight hours for them. You are not paid to conduct family business, or talk to your friends on the phone for long periods of time. You are not paid to take long breaks or extended lunches. You are paid to do the work your employer has hired you to do. It is only fair to give your company what they are paying for. Ask yourself this question: "If I were running my own company, would I pay me for what I am doing?"

Do not think for one minute that managers get off easy. In 2 Samuel 23:3, God tells David that the person in charge of other people must be just in his dealings with them. This means that managers must deal fairly with their employees. Do not require unpaid overtime. Do not have favorite employees, or employees who are constantly in your dog house. Treat each employee under you fairly and with respect.

For those in government leadership, this especially speaks to you. Remember, David was the King of Israel when God told him this. Judges, be just. Politicians, be fair. Do not let race, or economic status determine how you treat someone.

Everyone deserves a fair trial. Everyone is a constituent whom you are sworn to serve.

The Apostle Paul wrote to a young minister named Titus and gave him some things to look for in a minister (Titus 1:7-9). While Paul meant these requirements specifically for those who were to be ministers, I believe that some of them could apply to anyone who serves the public interest. Being just is among those qualifications.

Those who serve in church settings need to be just. They must treat everyone fairly. And so should those who work in food banks, soup kitchens, homeless shelters, and Salvation Army stores. Whether a paid staff member, or a volunteer, we should be fair when we are involved in helping the public.

As we go through life we are going to see injustice. God commands us not to be the cause of it.

God Is Love

The love of God is probably His best known characteristic, as well as the most misunderstood and misrepresented. We all like to think of God as love, but do we know what love really is? It is interesting to note that the Bible is unique in having a God of love. All other religions have gods who must constantly be appeased, and who look to their own interest. The idea of God being love is definitely more appealing than the alternative.

As we go through this chapter we are going to see what God has to say about love. We will look at how the Bible declares that the members of the Trinity are love, and then see how God has defined love. Hopefully by the time we are done we will have a clearer picture of what it means for God to be love.

God the Father

"God is love" is a direct quote of 1 John 4:8 and 16. The New Testament was written in Greek, and, without getting too technical, it bears looking at the original position of the words in the Greek manuscripts. The actual structure of the words in Greek is "the God love is." This structure is important in gaining the proper understanding of this phrase.

The article "the" is associated with the word "God." The Greek language is specific in identifying which words are to be paired with which articles. Because of the article, we find that this phrase cannot be reversed. It cannot be made to say that "love is God." Love is not the object of worship, nor is it the supreme power in the universe.

There is no article associated with the word "love." This means that love is a part of the nature of God. There is not a form of love possessed by God, instead His being is love. God is the ultimate perfection and embodiment of love. Just as He is the complete perfection of holiness and justice, God is completely and perfectly love.

1 John 4:7 tells us that "love is of God." God is the source of love. This would make sense as God is the only source of pure love in the universe. What John is trying to say with this phrase is that we can only experience true love when we get

our love from God. This is the thought that runs throughout this letter from the Apostle John.

John also tells us in his letter that God loves us so much that we are called His children (1 John 3:1). This is interesting. God does not call us His creation, or His handiwork, but He calls us His children. What an endearing and loving term that is. We are children whom God loves.

Throughout the New Testament God is portrayed as a God of love. This characteristic was emphasized and dwelt on more in the New Testament than in the Old Testament. It is that progressive revelation thing again. God displayed and revealed His love more in the New Testament, especially through the person of Jesus.

But, the Old Testament is not completely silent concerning the love of God. Deuteronomy 7:7 and 8 relates one of the speeches Moses gives to the people of Israel, telling them what God has commanded. In these verses God wants to make sure the people understand that He loves them. He chose them out of all the people groups of the world to be His people. They were not chosen because they were already a great nation. In fact they were slaves. And, He did not choose them out of sympathy either.

Long ago, God had chosen Abram to follow Him. We are never told what qualification of Abram prompted God to do this. God simply chose to love Abram and promised to make a great nation out of his heirs. But, not all of the heirs of Abram were loved by God and destined for developing a great nation. God chose to love Jacob over Esau his brother (Malachi 1:2,3). Again, there is no real reason for this choice. But God did uphold His promise to Abram by delivering his descendents from Egyptian bondage.

God the Son

Jesus constantly showed His love and compassion for people throughout His ministry. When it came to the final night with His disciples, before the crucifixion, Jesus wanted to make sure they understood that He loved them. We find this in John 15:9-17.

Jesus told the disciples that He loved them with the same love with which the Father had loved Him. This was a perfect love, and shows that the three persons of the Trinity are distinct enough to share love with each other. The love of God had been displayed to the disciples through Jesus.

The love of Jesus was so strong that Jesus considered them friends instead of servants. This was important in the thinking of that culture. Jesus was a teacher, and was considered a Master. The disciples were His followers, and were not to be treated as equals to the Master. Jesus, in His love, elevates these men to equality with Him as friends. Jesus thought highly of these men, and loved them. They were not people to command and rule, they were His friends.

Previous to calling the disciples His friends, Jesus tells them that the greatest love a man could have would be to die for His friends. Jesus, of course, died not only for His friends, but His enemies as well. Man can die for His friends, God dies for His enemies. But, the point is made with the disciples. Jesus is going to die for them because He loves them.

Finally, Jesus talks to the disciples about how He chose them. The disciples may have thought that they chose to follow Jesus, but they did not. Jesus invited each one of them to follow Him. He chose them before they decided to be a part of His life and ministry. Also, within all of the followers of Jesus, He only chose twelve to be within the inner circle. He only chose twelve to be His friends.

Jesus loves every person who would ever touch the face of this earth. He died for each person. Most reject this, many gladly accept it, but it is still true. John 3:16 tells us that God loved the whole world enough to have Jesus die to pay the price for their sin. Jesus loves each one of us enough to endure the pain of one of the most violent and horrific deaths in history, the Roman crucifixion. I do not believe there is anything else Jesus could do, or should have to do, to prove His love.

The Holy Spirit

Continuing in the book of John, we turn now to the Holy Spirit. What evidence do we find of His love? As Jesus is introducing the Holy Spirit to the disciples, He calls Him the Comforter (John 14:16,26;15:26;16:7). The Greek word used means an intercessor, counselor, advocate and comforter. It seems to me that, in order to give true comfort to someone, there must be a love there. The Greek word can also mean, "One who stands in the place of another." The Holy Spirit was to take the place of Jesus in the lives of the disciples. As such, there would be no reduction in the amount of love for the disciples. The Holy Spirit loves us as much as the Father and the Son. He has perfect love.

The Apostle Paul gives us some insight into the love of the Holy Spirit. He mentions how the Holy Spirit will pray for us when we are in trouble (Romans 8:26). The Spirit, Paul says, will groan while praying. To me this says that the Holy Spirit is empathizing with our hurts. Empathy comes from a love for the other person. The amount of empathy depends on the amount of love. The Holy Spirit groans deeply when we are hurting. His love is a deep, deep love.

So far we have just been able to infer that the Holy Spirit loves us. But, Paul removes all doubt in Romans 15:30. Paul asks the people to pray for him through the love of the Spirit. Paul had no doubt that the Holy Spirit loved him, in the same way Jesus does.

What Is Love?

Love is a choice.

God is pure love, and it is a part of His nature and being, but He still chooses who He will love. This was demonstrated in the passages we read in Deuteronomy 7 and John 15. Love must be chosen. There is no such thing as forced love. God cannot be forced to love anyone any more than we can be forced to love someone.

If someone were forced to love us it would not feel right. It would be mechanical. But, when someone chooses to love us, that makes it all the more special. Even though this is not a perfect example, let me try to explain it to you this way. Your sibling loves you (whether or not this is true, just play along). Your sibling is expected to love you because you are in the same family. That is alright, but not great. Real love comes when someone from outside your family chooses to love you. That is the person who makes you feel special because they have chosen to love you over others.

True love involves a choice. God chose to love us above any of the rest of His creation. Jesus did not die for plants or animals, or even angels. He died for you and me, and all of us humans. God is love, but He decides who He will love.

Love must have an object.

Love, like hate, must have an object toward which it is directed. Love must be connected to someone or something. We cannot simply say we love; we must identify what it is we love. This is true even for God. In this sense love is more than just an emotion or feeling; it is an action verb that needs a direct object in order to function properly.

We saw in the John 15 passage that the Father loves the Son. Continuing on, we find that the Father loved the Son, even before the foundation of the world (John17:24). The love between the members of the Trinity is an eternal one. It was in existence even before Jesus arrived in His human form. So, God has never been without an object of love.

This is interesting because God could have chosen to just love the members of the Trinity. He did not have to love us or anything else in order to experience love and be love. Remember, God is self-existent. He does not need anything else to complete Him, or to sustain Him. This is apparently true when it comes to love. I know it sounds egotistical that God loves Himself, but the love of God is not on an ego trip.

What really makes this exciting is that God did not need to love us. He chose to love us. He chose to go beyond Himself and make us the object of His love. God could have easily kept to Himself and never showed any kind of love toward us. But He did not do that.

God took a risk. Like you and I, God wants to be the object of love. He made us so that we might love Him. Understand that God does not need us to love Him, He simply desires it. We have already talked about love being a choice. The risk for God is that we would not love Him. Many people do not love Him; they do not even acknowledge His existence. God will never force anyone to love Him, but He chooses to never stop loving them.

Love is affection and correction.

When we think about love, we think about the affectionate side of it. We think about all the good things people should do for those they love, like gifts and good deeds. This is the way we want to think about the love of God. We get upset, and cannot seem to reconcile the concept of God punishing someone, because we have this one-sided view of love. There is an affectionate side of love, and it is great. But, there is also another side. I believe it is being called tough love.

Think about a parent with a child. There is appropriate affection shown the child, but what does a loving parent do when he sees that the child is about to do something that will hurt him? He tries to stop the child. Sometimes, in order to make the child understand that there are grave consequences to an action, the parent must discipline the child. Does spanking a child for crossing the street unattended mean that the parent does not love the child? No! The parent loves the child enough to give mild consequences to the child in order to keep them from suffering more dire consequences later.

Some may say that spanking and disciplining a child warps them, or is abusive. But, proper discipline is an act of love. The abuse comes from the parents who do not care what happens to their children so they do not discipline them.

They take the child's side in all disputes with teachers and authority figures. The child learns that he is always right and society is out to get him. I believe that allowing your child to grow up believing that there are no consequences to their actions is wrong. The child then becomes confused and bitter when he lands in jail. To not prepare your child for the reality of life is abusive.

God does punish people. But the punishment is mild compared to what they could ultimately end up with as a consequence. Remember that death is the ultimate consequence of sin. God will punish people to try to get their attention. He will give mild consequences so that a person may see that the action he is doing will lead to something worse. He does not want anyone to experience the ultimate penalty of complete and eternal separation from Him (2 Peter 3:9).

We should thank God that He does love us enough to discipline us. God is not abusive, He is caring. He wants what is best for us. He does not want us to have to experience negative consequences. In love, God gives us affection and correction.

The Bible defines love.

Love is one of the most difficult things to define, as are most emotions. The best we can usually do is give descriptions of what love is, or what it is not. The Apostle Paul gives us one of the greatest definitions of love ever found. As Paul is communicating with the church in Corinth he discovers that they have a problem with love. They do not seem to have any. In response, Paul writes them a letter and describes what love really is (1 Corinthians 13:4-8). Let us look at how God meets the standard set for love.

Love is patient. God is excruciatingly patient with us. He gives us chance after chance to love Him. Just look at the history in the Bible. In Genesis, God could have wiped out the human race with Adam and Eve, or at the time of the flood. Instead He simply removed Adam and Eve from the Garden of Eden, and saved Noah and His family on the ark. In Exodus, God could have done away with the people of Israel several times because they were rebelling against Him. But they were spared. As we read through the books of the prophets, we see God giving warning after warning for Israel to turn back to Him. The New Testament brings Jesus to die for our sin. Finally, in Revelation we see that God gives people chances to turn to Him all the way to the very end.

I cannot understand how God can be so patient. The human race would no longer exist if I were God. I would not exist if I were God. And yet, God patiently keeps trying to reach us. He faithfully brings people and situations into our lives to force us to look at Him. He patiently waits for us to choose to love Him.

Love is kind. Have you ever thought about all the good things God has done for us? There are too many to make a complete list, but let me mention a few. God gives us existence. He has provided this world for us to live in with air, animals, plants and beauty. Each day is new and full of possibilities. God uses His power and knowledge to help us, to make our life better.

Love does not envy. What would God have to be envious about? He has everything. Well, that is not entirely true. God does not have our love. If God were to be envious it would be in the fact that our love is placed somewhere besides Him. As we love other people, or things, or jobs instead of God, He could become envious of those things. But God does not come in and destroy those things, or force us to love Him. He allows us to make our own choice, and does not become envious when we decide to love something else.

Love does not boast and is not arrogant. Rightfully God could boast if He wanted to. He really is better than anyone else, so arrogance really could not define Him. But God is humble. The greatest act of humility was becoming one of His creations, and living among us, and then suffering death. Even in living a perfect life as a human, God did not boast. He never said, "I can do it, why can't you?" God has a right view of Himself and us. God is a lot of things, but He is not boastful and arrogant.

Love is not rude. God has class. He never acts in a way that is unbecoming to Him, or to the person He is dealing with. God is always there to listen intently to anything we say to Him. He does not rudely turn a deaf ear. There may be abruptness in His manner, depending on the urgency of the situation, but never rudeness.

Love is not self-seeking. All that God does is for us, and for our benefit. God is self-sufficient, not needing anything from us. With nothing to gain, He has everything to give. There is no need for God to be self-seeking.

Love is not easily angered. Yes, there are times in the Bible where we see God angry. But it was not easy to get Him there. Remember, God is patient, but there are limits. God does not have a hair trigger for a temper. The people of Israel were able to get Him angry several times while they were in the wilderness, but that was after much whining and complaining and unbelief in Him. God is slow to anger.

Love does not keep records of wrongs. Contrary to popular belief, God does not keep records of every wrong we do. The most important thing to God is having a relationship where we love Him. God does keep a record of our life, the good, the bad and the ugly. At the end of our days we will be shown the contents of these books, so that we can see the truth that we never allowed God to enter our life (Revelation 20:11-15). God does not sit there and point out every wrong thing we have done. He wants to forgive everything through the sacrifice Jesus made on our behalf.

Love does not rejoice in evil, but in truth. We have already seen that God is holy. There is no way that God could ever have a party celebrating evil. He would never contemplate doing evil toward us either. God lives in and for the truth. The truth is the proper definition of right and wrong. God always wants us to have good consequences for our actions, and points us in the direction of truth, not evil.

Love bears all things, trusts, hopes and endures. A person who loves another will go through anything with that person. In the wedding vows it is stated, "For better or worse, for richer or poorer." People who love each other can truly trust one another. Each person has hopes and dreams that the person they love will be happy. True love endures no matter what is thrown against it.

God loved us even while we were still against Him, and even hated Him (Romans 5:8). I would say that would be a rough time. God trusts us enough to allow us to make our own decisions, even when it comes to loving Him. God has dreams and plans for us, that we will be prosperous in life (Jeremiah 29:11). God's love lasts as long as He does. He always loves us, even when He has to allow us to face the final consequences of our actions.

Love never fails. God's love is strong and unwavering. It never diminishes, never weakens, it stays consistent. The pureness of his love means it never has to grow stronger, nor can it. The exhibition of God's love never causes it to be depleted, it is an unlimited supply. God loves each and every person on earth unfailingly.

Brush Strokes

When asked what the greatest commandment is, Jesus replied by quoting two Old Testament passages (Matthew 22:35-40). The first was Deuteronomy 6:5, "You are to love the Lord with all your heart, soul and mind." The second was Leviticus 19:18, "You are to love your neighbor as you would yourself." Jesus considered these two commandments about love to be the base of all of the other commandments in the Bible.

Jesus gave His disciples one commandment to follow: "Love each other like I have loved you" (John 15:12). It was very important to Jesus that His followers love each other. If they loved each other, then it would attract others to live that life style. Holiness is less of an effort if you simply love people.

There is no doubt that God wants us to love Him, and everyone else. This means that we follow the 1 Corinthians 13 pattern. We are to do what is best for others. We are to show affection, as well as correction. Do not let people do something that would harm them.

I do not believe I need to press this point. Everyone is looking for love. God says that we should choose to truly love everyone. Love is not easy, and loving everyone is next to impossible. But, God commands it, and He does not ask more than we can give.

The Mercy of God

God's holiness seems to empower two conflicting characteristics, love and justice. Justice demands that every action receive the appropriate reward or punishment. Love seeks to release us from the terrible penalties we must pay. When these two clash, it is the mercy of God that steps in to settle the dispute.

An Explanation of Mercy

What is mercy? To put it simply, mercy is not receiving a punishment you deserve. For example, the person convicted of a crime gets probation instead of the jail time he should have received. That is mercy from the judge. Mercy is when the person assigned to execute justice willingly decides to give a lesser sentence.

By definition, mercy cannot be bought or paid for through some good actions by the person receiving it. If mercy was paid for, then it would be deserved, and that would simply be justice fulfilled. Generally speaking, the price for mercy is paid for by the one giving it. Humanly speaking this is not always true, but it is when in reference to God's mercy.

Turning back to the example of someone getting parole instead of jail time, we see that society is the one who accepts the responsibility for this action. The judge represents us as a society when he renders his verdicts and sentences people. When he decides to let someone remain out of jail, society is the one who takes the risk of letting this person remain among them instead of isolating him from the population.

Maybe a different example would be better in explaining the fact that it is the person who gives the mercy who really makes the payment for it. Let us say that you have a car and that you have insurance on that car. As you are driving down the road another driver runs a stop sign and plows into your vehicle. The other driver does not have insurance, so your company pays you for the damages to your car.

You might think that is the end of it, but it is not. Your insurance company will now look to the uninsured driver to try to recover the money they paid to you to fix your car. The other driver owes the whole amount. They caused the accident and the resulting damages. Justice would demand that they repay the company 100% of their loss. But, if for some reason, the person was not able to pay the full amount, a deal might be made. The insurance company might settle for 75% or even 50% payment. To settle for a lesser amount would be showing mercy. The company would have to shoulder the rest of the loss. In other words, the company would be paying 25% to 50% of the money in order to extend mercy to this person.

God the Father

Moses, in speaking to the people of Israel while they were roaming around in the desert after fleeing Egypt, tells the people that God is full of mercy (Deuteronomy 4:31). He warns them that, if they start worshipping idols instead of God, they will lose the land God promised them and be scattered all over the known world. But, even if that happens, when they return to worshipping God, they will be forgiven. God will show mercy to them and fulfill the promise He has made to them by bringing them back into the land again.

The book of Psalms has a lot to say about the mercy of God. In Psalm 86 David records one of his prayers to God as a Psalm, or song. Within this short song David mentions the mercy of God five times. He either calls out for it to be given to him, or he declares the truth that it exists (Psalm 86:3,5,13,15,16).

It is in verses 5 and 15 that David makes the general statement that God is full of mercy. David reiterates this thought in Psalm 103:8. David believed that God had an overabundance of mercy within His being. The Apostle Paul also expressed this thought in his letter to the church of Ephesus (Ephesians 2:4).

David also shows us in Psalm 86 that God will have mercy on those who follow Him. His line of reasoning for asking for mercy from God begins in verse 2 where he says that he is holy and God's servant. In verse 5 David declares that God will show mercy to all who follow Him. His plea for mercy within this Psalm is based on this truth. David has also expressed this truth in greater detail within another Psalm. He says that the mercy of God encircles those who trust in God (Psalm 32:10). It is not just a burst of mercy that people experience who follow God, it is constantly with them and surrounding them.

Another view of God comes to the eyes of David because of a situation he got himself into. You can read what happened in 2 Samuel 11:1-12:14, but let us just give the short version here. David committed adultery and then had the husband murdered after his attempt to hide the affair failed. The prophet Nathan came to

David and told it like it was. David had gone against what God commanded, and he was going to suffer a penalty from it. David then writes Psalm 51 where his first words are "Have mercy on me God."

David already knew that God would show mercy to those who were following His commandments, but now he sees that God will have mercy on those who fail to obey a command and wish to ask forgiveness. David's son Solomon, who was the second child born to Bathsheba, with whom he had the affair, was a very wise man, and wrote many proverbs which have been recorded in the Bible. Proverbs 28:13 sounds like a lesson Solomon may have learned from his father David. If we try to hide our sin, we end up with trouble. But, if we will openly confess to God when we do something wrong, and stop doing it, we will receive mercy.

The prophet Isaiah said that God will give mercy and pardon to the person who acknowledges that he has done wrong, and turns away from that action. When this person asks for forgiveness, he will receive it from God (Isaiah 55:7). This message was especially important to the audience listening to Isaiah at the time. These were the people of Judah, the southern kingdom of Israel, who had worshipped other gods and had forgotten about God. Some of them may have been wondering if they had gone so far that God would never take them back. Isaiah says that God shows mercy to anyone who wants to come back to Him. What a relief and comfort to those people to hear those words.

Unfortunately it would take seventy years of captivity for them to turn back to following God, but the truth was there when they were ready to accept it. God was still merciful to them. Nehemiah was a Jewish leader who returned to Jerusalem, after the captivity suffered in Babylon and Persia, in order to rebuild the wall of Jerusalem. At the dedication of the wall, the Levites, who were a group in charge of operating the temple, gave a prayer for the people. Within this prayer they praise God for His mercy to their people by not destroying them for turning against Him, but by simply putting them into captivity so that they could return (Nehemiah 9:31).

Jesus gave us a parable about the mercy of God the Father which is recorded in Luke 15:11-32. It is referred to as the Parable of the Prodigal Son. Jesus says that there is a father who is rich. His youngest son decides he wants his independence; does not want to live under dad's rules anymore. So his father gives him the money he would inherit, and the kid takes off into the world to find himself. After much partying, and no working, the son finds out that his friends were there for him as long as the money held up. Soon he finds himself with no money, no friends, and no party. He ends up feeding pigs that are eating better than he is. Thoughts of his father and the grand place he left keep coming to mind. Even his father's servants were in better condition than he was. So, at last, he humbles himself and returns to his father to confess that he was wrong and did not deserve to be his son any more. As he is heading toward the house to beg his father to let him be a servant, his father sees him and runs out to meet him. With open arms the father welcomes him back as a son, not a servant.

God the Father is always watching for us to come to Him. He is always willing to show mercy to us, no matter how badly we have made a mess of things. God's love overcomes His justice to show us mercy. The Apostle Peter reflected this thought in his second letter when he says that God is not willing that anyone should have to perish by being separated from Him and dying spiritually, but wants everyone to leave their rebellion and return to Him (2 Peter 3:9).

God the Son

I said before that the price for mercy is paid by the one giving it. This is especially true in God's case. God's justice must be satisfied. If God extended mercy without the satisfaction of justice, then God would no longer be just. He would be letting us off easy, without the full punishment being paid. That is not justice. So, with every act of mercy given by God, He has made the full payment to justice for the penalty that should have been given to us. He did this through Jesus, God the Son.

The greatest display of mercy was the crucifixion of Jesus. There was no mercy in the men who crucified Him, but it was God's mercy unleashed as He fulfilled the demands of justice. As we saw when we discussed justice, the penalty for sin is death. That is what justice requires.

But, justice would also require that a person who had never committed a sin should never die physically, or suffer spiritual death by being separated from God. Jesus never sinned. He always listened to God and did exactly what God wanted Him to do. Jesus never did anything to cause negative consequences for Himself or others. Therefore, Jesus did not deserve to die. Actually, the only way Jesus could die is if He gave up His own life.

In the Old Testament the animal sacrifices temporarily paid the price for the sin of people. The animal had never done anything wrong, yet they died so the people did not have to. But the death of an animal can never equal the death of a human. Therefore, justice could never be completely satisfied. While physical death would always overtake a person, satisfying that part of justice, the spiritual death caused by the separation from God could not be satisfied. But, this was the part that the animal was meant to pay for, at least temporarily.

There existed a gulf in payment. Only the physical and spiritual death of a human who did not deserve it could pay the price to satisfy justice for everyone. This is what Jesus did. He physically died on the cross when He did not have to. And, according to His statement on the cross, there was actually a time when God did separate Himself from Jesus (Mark 15:34). I do not understand how God can separate from God, but He did. Jesus experienced both physical and spiritual death, paid the price of justice, and allowed the mercy of God to be given to everyone who would accept it. The love of God had paid the price for justice.

Earlier we spoke about how God shows mercy to those who will turn away from the bad things they are doing and start following God. Romans 5:8 tells us that the love of God is so strong in its desire to give mercy to us that, while we were still rebelling against God and not listening to Him, Jesus paid the price for us. In other words, God did not wait for us to ask Him for help in paying the price justice was demanding; He just went ahead and paid it for us anyway.

Jesus paid the price for God to be able to give mercy to everyone. So why is it that not everyone is free from paying the penalty that justice demands? Why are we not all headed toward an eternity in heaven? The only catch to God's mercy is that it be accepted by the person to whom it is given.

Actually, Jesus tackled this very topic as He spoke with Nicodemus, a religious leader who had come to ask questions (John 3:14-21). First, Jesus gives an example that Nicodemus would be familiar with. He refers to the time, during the wilderness wonderings of Israel, that God sent snakes into the camp to bite the people because they were complaining against God (Numbers 21:4-9). When the people wanted to ask forgiveness, God had Moses make a serpent out of brass and place it on a pole in the middle of the camp. Whoever was bitten could look on that brass serpent and be healed from the effects of the venom. Jesus uses this as a symbol of the death He would die on the cross.

Notice that the people had to look at the serpent in order to be healed. God could have healed all of them if He wanted, but He did not. When we talk about the steps for battling an addiction, whether it is drugs, alcohol, gambling, or anything else, the first step is always to admit you have a problem and need help. There is no point in extending mercy if the person does not own the bad action they did in order to need mercy. There will simply be no change in the person's life. If the people had simply been healed, then they would not have understood that their need was to follow God and stop rebelling against Him.

Jesus continues on in His talk with Nicodemus to say that only those who believe in Him will have eternal life (John 3:15,16). If we own the fact that we have sinned and deserve to pay the price for that sin ourselves, then we can look at Jesus and accept the fact that He paid the price for us. When we believe that Jesus has paid the price justice demands, then we can make that payment our own and accept His payment for our life. We see our need, and then we accept the mercy God has provided for us.

The people in the camp of Israel were already condemned to death when they were bitten by the snakes. The brass serpent did not condemn them to death, it saved their life. In the same way, we are already condemned to pay the penalty for our sin which justice demands. Jesus came so that those who saw their need could receive God's mercy, not to condemn those who refused to believe in Him (John 3:21).

Perhaps the greatest picture of what Jesus did for us in order to pay for our mercy is seen in a passage written hundreds of years before He stepped foot on the earth. Isaiah 53:4-12, gives a great picture of Jesus taking on our sin, and bearing the penalty Himself. It shows God pouring out the penalty and exacting justice on Jesus for all of our sin (iniquity). Finally it tells us that this sacrifice was accepted; that justice had been served. Jesus was resurrected from the dead, as justice for His perfect life was served on Him. His spiritual descendents would be many now that God was able to offer mercy.

God is perfectly willing to extend His mercy to those who see their need for it. Jesus has paid the price so that justice could be paid and mercy extended. In other words, Jesus paid the price demanded by justice, once and for all, for every single person. But mercy is only given to those who see their need and accept this.

The Holy Spirit

The Holy Spirit is all about mercy. Having mercy is a must if you are to be a comfort to people (John 14:16). The Holy Spirit was to be a comfort to the disciples as He helped them remember everything Jesus taught them. He would be able to show them how the mercy of God was manifested in Jesus.

And, Jesus shows us that the Holy Spirit's prime directive is to lead the world to mercy (John 16:8-11). We have looked at this passage before, but now it becomes much clearer. The Holy Spirit is to convict people of their sin. This is so that they will understand their need for mercy. Remember, a person cannot accept mercy until he sees the need for it. He is then to convince people of the penalty for sin brought about by justice. The news He spreads is about Jesus paying this penalty for them. Finally, He is to convince people that the judgment has already been set, and the only way out of it is through the mercy of God.

The Holy Spirit's job is to spread the word about the mercy God is extending toward each and every person. It is the mercy of the Spirit which fuels His passion in accomplishing this mission.

Summary

God the Father is full of love, which clashed with His justice. He devised a plan in order to extend mercy to those who would accept it. God the Son came to earth to live a perfect life and to die to satisfy the payment for sin demanded by justice. God the Holy Spirit now spreads the word to people, inviting them to accept the mercy of God.

Brush Strokes

God has gone to great lengths to be able to give us His mercy. We do not have to pay as high a cost in order to extend mercy to those around us. With this in mind, God has commanded that we show mercy to others.

We have already looked at one of the verses that commands us to love mercy, Micah 6:8. Yes, we are going to love mercy when we receive it, but God wants us to love mercy enough that we will give it to others. Displaying mercy should be an integral part of our moral fiber. It should become as natural as breathing.

Jesus tells us in Luke 6:36, that we should be merciful because God is merciful. God is our example when it comes to mercy, and this is very important. God teaches us that there is a price to be paid by the person giving the mercy.

So, when we plan on extending mercy, we need to ask ourselves if it is going to be worth the cost. Is there going to be too high of a price paid for not enough return? This is not selfish. There are instances where mercy would just cost too much. For instance, the wife whose husband physically abuses her should strongly consider the consequences of showing mercy. To show mercy to him in a way that would allow him to continue his abuse is too high of a cost.

God has also given us the example of setting a prerequisite for mercy. God shows mercy only to those who acknowledge they need it, and who ask for it. We should do the same.

As we looked at the scriptures earlier, we saw several references to God giving mercy only to those who followed Him, or who returned to a relationship with him. The scripture is not saying that these people were earning the mercy they received. Turning to God is an acknowledgment of the need for mercy, and is the first step in being able to receive mercy. It is also an action which shows a change of heart and attitude toward the previous wrong actions that were being done. This is a first step in a change of behavior.

Setting this prerequisite will keep us from getting run over by other people. Lessening the sentence of a criminal just to show mercy is not smart. The criminal must first show a true remorse for his actions, and then honestly acknowledge his need for help. In the previous illustration of the abusing spouse, the husband must know that what he is doing is wrong. Then he must honestly show signs of desiring a change in his behavior. If he wants mercy after those things are in place, it can be granted.

There is another side of mercy. So far we have just looked at lessening the punishment of those who do wrong. But, God also has a heart for those who are poor, or orphans, or having trouble in some area of life. Extending mercy to these people is simply a matter of helping them overcome their circumstances. We are not to make their burden heavier.

Once again the criteria are in play for when and how to show mercy. These people must acknowledge their need for mercy, and have the desire to take action to improve their condition. If a person is capable of working, but just not wanting to work, then the merciful thing to do is let him starve for a while until he understands the benefits of work. But, if a person is willing to work and just cannot find a job, help him look for a job, and help with his finances as much as possible. That is mercy.

We are commanded to show mercy to other people. But, it is not a command to let people walk all over us, or to turn our backs on delving out real punishment. Even God is careful about who He gives mercy to.

A final verse we will look at is found in Hosea 6:6. God is talking to the people of Judah again, after they have spent a long time worshipping other gods. He tells them that He would rather have them seeking mercy, than to see them making meaningless sacrifices to Him. In other words, the ritual of the sacrifice was there, but the heart and attitude desiring mercy was not. The people's relationship with God was nothing more than a pretentious sham.

For the people God was speaking to in Hosea, the sacrifices had changed in meaning. They were so caught up in their pagan rituals that they came to see the sacrifices to God as being the same as to the false gods. Sacrifices were being made to try to appease God, like they would do for some false god, instead of out of a desire for mercy from the punishment of sin. These people forgot that the sacrifices were for their benefit, not God's. God did not need the sacrifice for any reason. It was the people who needed the sacrifice in order to temporarily satisfy the demands of justice for their sin.

In our relationship with God, we must always acknowledge our need for mercy. When we do not acknowledge our need for mercy, we change the relationship into something that was not intended. We may begin to see God as a buddy who can give us anything we want. Or, we may see God as someone who needs to be appeased in order to like us.

We are commanded to have mercy as an integral part of our life. It should be a part of our dealing with others, and with God. We should seek to receive mercy from God, and give it to others.

God Is True

In this chapter we will be discussing what is at the foundation of every good relationship. Truth must be the base. Without truth there is no trust, and without trust there is no relationship. God wants us to have a relationship with Him. That is why He paid the price for mercy. So, does God lie, or does He always speak the truth? What does the Bible have to say about God being true?

God the Father

During his farewell speech to Israel, Moses launched into a song he had written about God. No one in the Old Testament knew God more intimately than did Moses. Early on in the song Moses identifies God as being a God of truth (Deuteronomy 32:4). In all of His experience with God, Moses found that God never lied to him. God always did what He promised; He never said one thing and then did another. Moses trusted God and declared Him to be a being of truth.

Solomon gave a blessing to the people at the dedication of the temple in Jerusalem. Within that blessing he mentioned the fact that God had fulfilled all of the promises that Moses had recorded about Israel (1 Kings 8:56). God had been true to His word, and had not lied about anything.

The writers of the New Testament were able to look back over the years and see with clearer vision if God had really fulfilled His promises and kept His word. When it comes to knowing the Old Testament promises, the Apostle Paul was probably the most educated person who wrote in the New Testament. He was highly trained by one of the best teachers of his day in what the Old Testament scriptures said. He came to one conclusion. God is true (Titus 1:2).

God the Son

The Gospel of John was written by one of Jesus' closest companions, and gives us a clear picture and description of Jesus. The Apostle John begins his book by declaring Jesus as God. In John 1:14, John declares that Jesus is full of truth. In verse 17, John says that truth came by Jesus. This was the truth about God and His relationship with people.

Jesus declared Himself to be the truth (John 14:6). He was saying that He is the only One who has the truth about God. That is a strong statement, especially if it was found to be false. However, nothing in the life or words of Jesus would suggest that this statement was anything but true. Jesus is the truth of God in human flesh.

The Holy Spirit

Three times Jesus calls the Holy Spirit the Spirit of truth (John 14:17; 15:26; 16:13). These were all spoken during His final talk with the disciples, as He is explaining about the coming of the Holy Spirit. I do not see any need for belaboring the point that that Holy Spirit is true.

Defining Truth

I believe we could define truth as the accurate representation of things as they really are. In other words, real truth is not telling what we think or believe to be real; it is stating exactly what is real. We could be wrong if we state what we believe to be real, and that would be a distortion of the truth. A lie is when we state something to be true when we know it to be false. It is only when we accurately represent things as they really are that we have the truth.

We have seen that the Bible has declared that God is truth. But, could God ever not tell the truth? Let us put our definition to the test against God. Does God always accurately represent things as they really are?

First, can God lie? Can He intentionally say something is true when He knows it to be false? No. God is holy, and therefore cannot lie. A lie would create a negative consequence. It would destroy our trust in Him. Just one lie would cause us to always wonder if He were lying to us again. It would destroy our relationship with Him and we could end up spending eternity without Him. The lie would be sin, which would destroy His holiness, and in effect, His entire moral character. He would become like us. God cannot do that. He must be true to His character (2 Timothy 2:13; Hebrews 6:18).

Second, can God unknowingly distort the truth? In other words, is there some way that God could make a mistake and unwittingly misrepresent something? Let me give you an example of what this would look like for me. Let us say that I loan my car to a friend. I tell my friend they will have no problems making it to their destination and back with the amount of gas that is in the car. Twenty minutes later the friend is walking toward me and looking very upset. The car ran out of gas. I did not know that the gas gage was stuck, or that there was not as much gas as I thought. I did not lie because I was going on the facts available to me; but, I did not tell the truth either. I unwittingly misrepresented what was real. Could God ever fall into that trap?

We have learned that God is omniscient. He knows everything. There is no way that some detail could possibly slip by Him and He accidentally distort the truth. There is no way God can be fooled into thinking that something is true when it is not. He would have known the gas tank was almost empty. If God distorts the truth it is not from a lack of knowledge. Therefore, He would be lying, and we have already covered that.

God can never lie. He always keeps his promises. What He says He is going to do, He accomplishes. It may not always be on our time table, or even the way we think it should be done, but God always comes through.

Examples of Fulfilled Promises

The best way we learn to trust people is through time and experience. We do not come up to a stranger and trust them completely. There must be time to get to know them, and to view their record for telling the truth. What I want to do now is to look at some of God's record that is recorded in the Bible. Has He made good on promises He made to people in the past? If He has, then there is reason to believe that He will continue to do so; if He has not, then He is a liar and cannot be trusted.

Abram (Abraham)

Abram was a man who lived with his family in Ur of the Chaldees, which is in modern day Iraq. He was wealthy, and apparently knew about God. When Abram was seventy five years old, God told him to leave the land his family owned and go where He was going to lead him (Genesis 12:1-4). Years before, Abram's father, Terah, had moved the family out of Ur and into Haran to start a new life. This may have made it easier for Abram to move, especially after the passing of his father.

As God called Abram to move, He promised him that a great nation would come from him. He also promised to bless Abram and make his name great. This may have been a little hard for a seventy five year old man and his sixty five year old wife, who had no children, to believe. God was promising to give him children?

When Abram reached the land of Canaan, God told Abram that his descendants would inherit that land (Genesis 12:7). This is modern day Israel. Abram believed God then. But, when Abram was ninety nine years old, God came to him again to promise him a child. This time, Abram laughed at God (Genesis 17:17). His wife, Sarai, was ninety years old, way past child bearing years, and he was ninety nine, almost one hundred. But God promised that Sarai would have a child within the year (Genesis 17:21). God showed He was serious about this promise by changing Abram's name to Abraham (Genesis 17:5). Abraham means "father of a great multitude." Sarai's name was changed to Sarah, which means "princess" (Genesis 17:15).

So, did God fulfill His promises to Abraham to give him a child through Sarah and land to pass down as an inheritance? Look at Genesis 21:1-8. That same year, Sarah gave birth to Isaac, just like God said would happen. Isaac was the father of Jacob and Esau (Genesis 25:19-26). Jacob's name was changed to Israel (Genesis 32:24-28). Jacob had twelve sons which became the patriarchs of the tribes of Israel (Genesis 35:22-26). Jacob lived in the land of Canaan (Genesis 37:1). After over 400 years of living in Egypt, the descendants of Israel came back to Canaan and retook the land. Today, the land of Israel still exists.

As we read through the story of Abraham and his family in Genesis, we see that other people groups were also established from Abraham. Abraham had another child named Ishmael, who was born from one of his servants. This was the beginning of the Arab family. Esau, Jacob's brother, also had children which grew into tribes in the region.

Against what seemed like impossible odds, God kept His promise to Abraham.

King David

2 Samuel 7:1-17 finds King David wanting to build a temple for God. But God did not want David to build a temple for Him. Instead, God tells David that his son would build the temple. He also promises that, as long as there is a king on the throne of Israel, it would be one of David's descendents.

This is fantastic news to David. He is disappointed that he will not be allowed to build the temple for God, but he is thrilled that his children will continue to rule. The king of Israel before David was Saul. Saul did not follow God, and because of that, God cut off his line from ever taking the throne again. David was relieved to hear that this would not happen to his family.

Did God make good on His promise to David? Solomon, David's son who followed David on the throne of Israel, did build the temple (1 Kings 6:1). There was always a descendent of David on the throne of Judah, the southern kingdom of Israel after the civil war split the country. God did keep his promise to David.

Jeremiah

Jeremiah was a prophet in Jerusalem just prior to its fall to Babylon. God told Jeremiah that the destruction was about to come on Judah, and they would be carted away into captivity in Babylon. And, God promised Jeremiah that the people would only be captive in Babylon for seventy years (Jeremiah 25:11-12).

The prophet Daniel read the words of Jeremiah and knew that the end of the captivity was close (Daniel 9:2). Daniel was a Jewish prophet who was captive in Babylon. He looked forward to the time when the Jews could return home.

God was true to His word. Seventy years after the start of the captivity, Babylon had fallen to the empire of Media-Persia. Cyrus, the Persian king, declared that the Jews could return to their homeland and rebuild their temple. Years later a group would return with Nehemiah to rebuild the wall of Jerusalem. Though the people of Israel were not an independent state again until 1948, God did uphold His word that they would return after only seventy years in captivity.

Jesus

We have seen that in His final words to the disciples, Jesus promised to send them the Holy Spirit (John 14-16). This promise was completed in Acts 2:1-4. The disciples, around 120 of Jesus' followers, were sitting in the upper room. Without warning there was a roaring sound like a strong wind, only nothing was being blown around. Little tongues of flame appeared above each of their heads, and they began to speak foreign languages. The Holy Spirit had arrived to live within each one of them.

Something to Think About

Jesus also made a promise which has yet to be completed. In John 14:1-3, Jesus promises to return to get us so that we can be with Him forever. That was the whole purpose of Him coming to earth to die. He wanted to pay the price so that mercy could be extended and we could have an eternal relationship with Him. Since God is true to His word and keeps His promises, we have to believe that this promise will also be kept.

Brush Strokes

We are not to tell lies about our neighbors (Exodus 20:16). That is the ninth commandment. Apparently telling the truth is a big deal to God since it made His top ten list. Lying about someone is detrimental to the person who was lied about, and to the person who lied. The lie will do damage to a person's reputation, even when it is discovered that it is a lie. And, when it is discovered it is a lie, it does damage to the liar's reputation. It does not foster trust within a community.

Of course we are speaking of someone who intentionally lies. But, remember, there is another way of not telling the truth. If we unintentionally spread misinformation about someone, we have not told the truth about them. Gossip, unless verified as absolute truth, is the spread of an untruth, or lie. It is rare that gossip gets verified as truth. Gossip probably does more damage than an outright lie. The danger with gossip is that there is usually a little truth mixed in with the lie to make it believable. So, separating the fact from the fiction becomes a tedious job that few people take the time to accomplish. Therefore, the lie is harder to refute, and the victim's image remains tarnished at best.

Jesus touched on the subject of truth during one of His sermons. It was probably one of His stock sermons to the people, and it is recorded in Matthew 5-7. Within this passage Jesus tells the people to stop taking elaborate oaths that have loopholes. Let your word be your bond (Matthew 5:33-37). When you say that you are going to do something, do it. Let your yes mean yes, and your no mean no. Tell the truth and keep your promises. Do not try to find excuses for why you could not keep a promise, or why you need to break a promise. Just tell the truth.

Lies and deceptions are something almost everyone complains about and almost everyone does, in one form or another. We do not like to see it in politicians, or coworkers, or our children, but it is there. To realize that the person we see every morning in the mirror also does it is a bit discomforting as well. Is it any wonder that we have a hard time getting along in communities when we cannot trust each other?

God wants us to tell the truth for a reason; it is easier on all involved. You are probably thinking what I am right about now. What about the white lies we tell to make people feel better? Those have their own consequences, which are usually milder than what God was addressing in the commandments and in Jesus' sermon. To tell someone that a dress looks nice when it is really ugly is one thing; spreading the rumor the person is a cross dresser is another. Spreading untruth that would be detrimental to the person being talked about is wrong and hurtful. What if it were being said about you?

The command not to lie fits in with the command to love our neighbor as we love ourselves. You would not want to spread hurtful rumors about yourself, why would you want to spread rumors that would hurt others?

Telling the truth is usually hard work. But, it must be done if there is going to be any kind of trust in this world. God understood that, and made it one of His top ten priorities. It should be one of ours.

Section Summary

In this section we saw the colors added to the portrait of God. We began with the purity of the holiness of God. Like spirit is for the physical characteristics, holiness is the moral characteristic from which all the others flow. It is the most prominent color in the portrait of God.

We found that the definition for holiness was not keeping everything bad away from you, but instead, it is embracing what is right to the exclusion of what is wrong. God is so pure in His goodness, and so full of goodness that anything bad has no room to even leave a mark on Him.

Justice showed us why the penalty for sin is death. Whenever we listen to someone else, and act on their definition of right and wrong instead of to God, it leads to death. Justice demands payment. The holiness of God powers His justice. It will not allow anything but the proper penalty for wrong and the proper reward for right.

To contrast justice, we looked at love. Holiness also empowers love, so that it is completely pure. We looked at the characteristics of love found in 1 Corinthians 13. But, the most important thing to remember about the love of God is that it is not a romantic love. God's love contains both affection and correction. When it comes down to it, God loves us by always doing what is best for us, even at His own expense.

The struggle between love and justice was bitter until holiness stepped in to referee. The result was mercy. Justice demanded that we die to pay the price for our sin; love desired that we live. The result was that God became a man, lived a perfect life, and satisfied the payment justice demanded for us. God bought the right to extend mercy to us.

God has promised to extend this mercy to us. He has also promised that, if we will accept His gift of mercy, we will be able to have a relationship with Him for eternity. These promises would be meaningless if God did not always keep His promise. God is true, and He cannot lie about anything. To break a promise is to lie.

What wonderful colors we have found as we have looked into the moral characteristics of God. With holiness as their base, the other characteristics seem to explode in vibrancy. In the next section we will look at some characteristics which blend the colors together.

THE FINAL TOUCHES

THE COMBINATION
CHARACTERISTICS

◆

WISDOM
SOVEREIGN
UNCHANGEABLE

God Is Wise

We are launching into the final section in our look at the portrait of God. In this section we will study three characteristics of God which are either dependent on both the physical and moral attributes, or significantly affect those characteristics. Because of their interaction with the physical and moral characteristics, it is difficult to pigeonhole these final three attributes into one or the other category. They are a pure blend of colors.

Let us begin with wisdom. The topic of wisdom seems to be very important in the Bible. The book of Proverbs is wholly devoted to the subject. God must count this as one of His important characteristics to place that much emphasis on it. At the same time, it is a characteristic that He wants to see us develop.

Defining Wisdom

Wisdom can be defined as the proper use of knowledge. That seems like a simple definition, but on further examination, it is not so simple. First, there must be knowledge. Whether we like it or not, we are constantly gaining knowledge. We learn about people, how things work, where places are, and even learn about that person in the mirror. This has been deemed the information age because we have unprecedented access to any and all kinds of information. There seems to be no shortage in the supply of knowledge.

Second, there must be a use of that knowledge. I can learn how a lawn mower works; how the gas combusts to power the engine, which turns the blades to cut the grass. But, my grass would be three feet tall, and my neighbors greatly upset, if I did not apply that knowledge to actually using the mower to cut my grass. It is important for knowledge to be used in order for it to have any real significance.

Finally, the knowledge must be used properly. It is not enough just to use knowledge, it must be used properly. The lawn mower is not to be used as a fan, nor is it to be used to chop up your neighbor's flowerbed. The proper, and wise, use of a lawnmower is to mow your lawn. When the knowledge is used is also important to the proper use of knowledge. Trying to mow my lawn in winter is not the right time. Knowledge that is used improperly leads to bad results.

Wisdom always leads to good results. In fact, wisdom allows God to choose the best course of action in order to achieve the most beneficial result.

With this definition we can see that it is possible for someone to have a great deal of book knowledge, and still not be wise. One of the characters in the book of Job said that great men are not always wise (Job 32:9). The person who knows the benefits of a healthy diet, and yet continues to eat unhealthy food, is smart, but not wise. If a person has had a heart attack and understands their need for exercise, but still does not do it, that person has knowledge, but no wisdom. It is possible to be very smart, but not wise.

Wisdom and the Characteristics of God

In this section we are going to look at things in a little different way. Up to now, I have been dividing up the members of the Trinity and showing how each one possesses the appropriate characteristic of God. I believe that we should know by now that each member has the same characteristics by virtue of being God. So, unless there is some interesting point to be made, or fact to be shown, I will no longer separate the members. When I speak of God I am including the Father, the Son, and the Holy Spirit.

Omniscience is the most obvious characteristic of God associated with wisdom. The base of wisdom is knowledge. Without knowledge it is difficult to make decisions. God knows everything, including all of the possibilities stemming from a decision. With his omniscience, nothing gets past God. He is never blind sided by an unexpected turn of events, or cornered by unforeseen consequences.

The ability to use this knowledge comes from His omnipotence and omnipresence. God has the power and ability to do anything. Whatever needs to be done for a proper outcome, God has the resources to accomplish it. But, resources are no good if they are not where they are needed most.

During the D-Day invasion, the Allies feared the German tank divisions could repel the whole operation. However, because of errors in the German leadership, the tanks either never engaged, or were so late as to be ineffective. God never has that problem. His resources are always available right where they are needed, and when they are required. He is omnipresent, so there is no place in the universe that can be isolated enough for Him to not be able to engage the proper ability to accomplish the task.

It is the moral attributes of God (His holiness, justice, love, mercy and truth) that allow God to properly use His knowledge. Without the moral aspect, God could misuse His knowledge and thwart wisdom. But God is wise because He has the moral base to properly use His infinite knowledge. Holiness is the preeminent factor in all of the moral attributes, as well as in the moral side of wisdom. However, wisdom is needed in order to dispense justice, love and mercy. So, there is a definite merging and reliance between wisdom and the moral characteristics of God.

Examples of God's Wisdom

The Bible tells us that God used His great wisdom when He created the universe (Psalm 104:24; Proverbs 3:19; Jeremiah 10:12). Scientists all agree that there is an order and design to the universe. Those who held to the Big Bang Theory for the origin of the universe still had to admit that there is an order to things. Science is all about discovering that order.

It was the wisdom of God that placed all of the stars and planets in this universe. The earth is just the right distance from the sun because of the wise planning by God. A little closer and everything would burn, a bit further and everything would freeze.

God planned for the purification of the air through the plants, and the purification of the water through the water cycle. As plants breathe in carbon dioxide, they take out the carbon and exhale oxygen. Animals and humans do the opposite. Impure water is evaporated, leaving the impurities on the ground to help make dirt. Then the water returns to the ground as rain, more pure than when it left.

There are a variety of eco systems around the world, each one containing animals specifically suited for their environment. God used His wisdom to keep us from being bored with our surroundings here on earth. There are tall mountains where very little life exists, but provide absolute pristine beauty. Antarctica and the North Pole are frozen waste lands that still provide a habitat for penguins and polar bears. The lush green jungles of the rain forests provide unique, and sometimes scary, creatures. The plains of Africa are populated by lions and tigers and elephants. Untold species of fish live in the ocean. We probably have yet to discover some of the species that live in the very deepest part of the oceans where the pressure is great and light never penetrates.

With wisdom God gave us day and night, and the changing seasons (Psalm 74:16,17). Ask those in Alaska, or the Arctic Circle, how it is to have sunlight twenty four hours a day, or darkness for twenty four hours. It is not pleasant. If God had made it constantly daylight, we would never have any down time. Constant darkness would have made it depressing and hard to see. But, God gave us both day and night for most of the earth during most of the year.

Can you imagine how boring it would be if we only had one season? We would bake if all we experienced was summer. Nothing would ever grow if it was always winter. Fall with its changing leaves and cooler temperatures would not be as appreciated, and the drab colors would eventually depress us. The flowers of spring would be nice, but the constant rain it would bring would be a bit of a downer. Too much of one thing is just not good. Wisdom says that variety is the key to replenishment of body and soul. And God made the seasons so that we could be replenished as we moved through the year.

So, God used wisdom as He created this universe. He also used wisdom in His plan to pay the price demanded of us by justice. The Apostle Paul tells the church in Ephesus that the church was to spread the news that justice had been paid through the wise plan of God being carried out (Ephesians 3:1-12, especially 10-12). Omniscience determined the method of payment. A morally perfect man had to die. Wisdom determined how the plan was to be enacted.

It was wisdom that determined when the best time would be for God to step into human history and die for the sin of mankind (Romans 5:6, Galatians 4:4,5). Had God come earlier in Israel's history, while they were still worshipping other gods, Jesus would have just been passed over as a leader of a new religion. No need for death there. A little later and Israel was disbursed, no nation existed again until 1948. By that time the world was reeling from the effects of two barbarous world wars, and no one would have paid much attention to just one more man preaching about peace. Jesus stepped into human history at just the right time. The cruelty of crucifixion, mixed with the tense nationalistic and political environment, provided the perfect opportunity for an innocent man to die.

Wisdom also understood that placement was important. God gave Abraham the land of Canaan, what we call Israel. Strategic location is a gross understatement when it comes to this piece of land. It sits at the connecting point of the two major continents of the ancient world, Africa and Asia. All commerce and travel between the two land masses and their respective world powers, had to go through Israel. That is why every conquering power from Babylon, to Persia, Greece and Rome, all wanted possession of that land. It was truly a crossroads of the world.

For God to walk the earth on that particular plot of ground was wise. From there the word of Jesus was able to spread to all the known continents at the time. By land Africa and Asia were easily reached, and Europe was available by land and sea. Israel was still a central location in trade and travel.

At the time, the Greek society had given rise to debate and logic, while still holding onto the belief of gods and goddesses. It was a world that could understand the logic of God's plan, and still believe in God. Within this context, along with the Jewish system of synagogues, the message was easily dispersed intellectually. The Roman system of roads made travel much easier for the message to be sent geographically. It would have been more difficult to reach the message to the world from the Far East, instead of from the Middle East.

Television is a good medium for getting a message out to a large number of people quickly. But, television is highly impersonal. God's plan is a message that is extremely personal, both to the person telling it, and to the person listening. The Greek and Jewish systems of relating information through oratory and debate were very personal, and played right into the spreading of the message God has for each individual. I cannot prove this, but, I believe that God's message would have died out if He had to rely on radio or television to send it in those early days. Even today it is the personal touch of neighbors speaking to neighbors, and churches meeting on a weekly basis that really communicates the message of God. Radio and television are great tools, but personal communication is always best. That is why Paul's ability to travel to the different churches worked so well.

Wisdom also had to decide if the price to be paid was going to be too high. God could have looked at what He was going to have to do and decided not to even create people. Or, He could have destroyed us all in the flood, and no one would have known any better. Justice and love, mercy and holiness, battled it out as wisdom refereed. In the end, God decided that the cost was not too great for Him to endure. His love for us was so strong that He would rather die for us than have us live without Him. The price was high for God, but higher for us if we were left to pay it on our own.

The wisdom of God is absolutely astounding. Every day His wisdom guides events and people, and we do not even realize it.

<u>God the Son</u>

There is no doubt that Jesus was wise when He walked this earth. We read through Matthew chapters 5 through 7, and we see Him take the religious ritualism of His day and debunk it. He makes the worship of God personal, and relational. He took the outward religious actions and made them matters of the heart and attitude. Knowledge brought out all the laws and sacred rituals, but the wisdom of Jesus brought out the person of God to meet with the worshipper.

One of my favorite passages in the Bible is Matthew 22:15-46 (Also found in Mark 12:13-37 and Luke 20:20-44). It is the final week of Jesus' ministry before the crucifixion, and He is teaching in the temple. The religious leaders all decide to gang up on Jesus to try to outsmart Him. They want Him to say something wrong so they can either get the Romans to kill Him, or the people to stone Him.

Three times the religious leaders hit Jesus with questions. The first on taxes was wisely answered. The second on a rule in the Mosaic Law was also wisely answered. The third, concerning the greatest commandment, was wisely answered. Then came the final strike against the religious men. Jesus asked them a very wisely crafted question. "Whose son is the Christ?" The answer was the son of David, everyone knew that, but they had walked into a trap. Jesus then follows up His question. "How could the high King David ever call one of his heirs Lord, or king, over him?" The answer of course is that the Christ would have to be God in order to be above David on the throne of Israel. But the religious leaders would not admit it.

No one asked Jesus any challenging questions after that. I love that passage because these smart, egotistical, pompous religious men went into a fight against wisdom unarmed. For all of their knowledge, they were not wise. It was their lack of wisdom that caused them to hate Jesus instead of recognizing who He really was. They lost badly, and went away licking their wounds. (Sometimes my sense of justice overcomes my sense of love and mercy. That is why I love this passage.)

Brush Strokes

In the Old Testament the book of Proverbs is considered a wisdom book. It is full of wise sayings which Solomon collected. Solomon was no slouch. He was the wisest man ever to walk the face of the earth, except for Jesus. In the New Testament the book of James is considered to be the leader in wisdom. We will look at passages from both books, but mostly from James.

We defined wisdom as the proper use of knowledge. So, let us take the definition apart and see how the Bible relates it to us. As far as the Bible is concerned, the foundation of wisdom is knowledge. Just like the omniscience of God is the base of His wisdom, our knowledge is to help us make wise decisions.

Proverbs 1:7 tells us that the root, or principal part of knowledge, is a fear or respect for God. If we respect God, we will follow His ways, we will learn His rules for how the universe and life work best. Knowing these things affects how we perceive or process other information we receive. It gives us a grid in which to sort out what is true information, and what is false.

Knowledge must include the understanding of whether information is true or not. If we read somewhere that you can work with electricity as long as you wear rubber soled shoes, we need to know if that is true or not before we begin sticking our finger into a plugged in light socket. False information could be deadly. It is not enough to know something; you must know if it is true or false. If we respect God, then we trust Him to tell us what is true and not give us false information.

The first step in us being wise is to respect God enough to have a relationship with Him. We must be able to trust that what He tells us is true. Otherwise, we begin building our conclusions on false information.

James 1:22-25 touches on the matter of using knowledge. James tells us to look at the word of God and then do it. Don't just sit there, act on what you know to be true. He gives an example of someone who looks in the mirror and sees their messed up hair, stained teeth, dirty clothes, and worn out shoes. This relates to us looking at what God says is the truth about us and other things. The person who sees what a mess they are, but goes out in public without fixing anything, is unwise. This is the same as knowing the truth but deciding to follow the false knowledge of someone else instead. The wise person acknowledges the truth found in the mirror, and does something to correct his appearance before he goes into public. This person has a good day as people do not try to shun him thinking he is a panhandling bum. Acting on the truth we learn from God is the second step for us to be wise.

Finally we come to the part about properly using the knowledge we have gained. The knowledge of God is absolute truth, and we must act on it. But, too many people act improperly. The Crusades and the Inquisition would be two good examples. But, people still act improperly in relation to the truth of God. Many people try to make religion out to be all about rituals, ceremonies, and icons. They think a person has to worship in a certain place, or at a certain time.

James follows up his comments about using knowledge with a few words about using it properly (James 1:26-27). He says that people can talk a good game when it comes to being religious, but here is what a person will do if they really have a relationship with God through Jesus, and are following His true knowledge. They will look out for the fatherless, help out the widows, and generally help those who are less fortunate and in need. Jesus put it in about the same way in Matthew 25:31-46. He says that when the end of days comes, and He is judging people, He will ask them the important question of how they used their knowledge. Did they feed the hungry, take care of the sick, or visit the prisoner? Did they show the love they knew to be true about God to those around them?

God does not give us His true knowledge in order for us to make rules and regulations which hurt other people. He gives us knowledge of Himself so that we can be more like Him. He gives us knowledge of His love, mercy, holiness, justice, and truth so that we can have those qualities and give them to others. That is true wisdom.

Jesus gives us a good picture of our definition of wisdom as He ends up His most famous sermon (Matthew 7:24-27). He says that there were two men who knew how to build houses. One was wise and dug down to set his house on a foundation of rock. The other was lazy and just built on top of the ground in the sand. When the storm came through, the house with the foundation of rock held firm, but the house on the sand was destroyed.

Jesus said that those who hear His words (knowledge) and follows them (used properly) are like the man who built his house on the rock. But, those who hear His words (knowledge) and do not follow them (used improperly) are like the guy who built on the sand. The word of Jesus is the rock foundation, and that is why the house stood. Both men heard the word of Jesus. The difference was in the application. It is following the word of Jesus that places you on the rock foundation. Deciding to not follow the knowledge of Jesus places you on the sand.

One final thought from James concerning wisdom. Maybe you are thinking that you cannot be wise, or that God really does not place a high priority on this following of His word as the base for wisdom. Look at James 1:5-8. James says that if you lack wisdom, you do not think you have any, then ask God and He will supply you with it. Wisdom is so important that God does not want anyone to have to be without it. He wants to freely make it available. Just ask.

But, look at what else James says. You have to have faith in God when you ask. In other words, you must believe that what God says is true. You must have a respect and trust in God.

James talks about a double minded man, or a person who is trying to look both directions at the same time. This type of person picks and chooses what he wants to believe about God. He only believes what he wants to. The things he does not like, he fills in with the knowledge someone else has given to him. This person does not have a full trust in God to tell him the truth. That means this person will never be wise because his foundation of wisdom, knowledge, is tainted. He should not expect anything in the way of wisdom from God. God will not waste His time trying to give wisdom to someone who does not believe what He tells them.

God wants us to be wise. The foundation of wisdom is knowledge, and knowledge comes from a respect and trust for God to tell us the truth. We must put into practice the knowledge God has given us, and it must be practiced in an appropriate manner. Being wise is hard work, but God has promised to help us. All we have to do is ask.

God Rules

I fail to see how anyone could say that God does not rule the universe, or at least has the right to rule the universe. The old fashioned term for this is sovereignty. The kings and queens of Europe were sovereign. They had the right to rule over their countries and territories. God has the right to rule over the universe. The term sovereign is not found in the Bible. God's sovereignty is denoted in the use of the word Lord. This word is found consistently throughout the Bible in relation to God.

God's physical characteristics make Him the most powerful and knowledgeable being in the universe. He is the only being who can be in all places of His realm at the same time. If God had the right to rule simply with these characteristics, He could be a tyrant. But, his physical characteristics are ruled by His moral attributes. He is holy, so He can do nothing that would intentionally hurt someone else. He is just, which means He is fair in His dealings with His subjects. He loves His subjects, and thinks of their welfare over His own desires. His mercy is extended to everyone who will accept it. God uses wisdom in all He does. He is the ultimate ruler.

This characteristic of God, the fact that He is in charge and in control of everything, is very controversial. It is hard to reconcile how a good God who is in control of everything could allow evil to be present. Remember when we talked about justice? We said that God is fair, but there are some things that fall under the heading of life happening. I said then that we would discuss the issue of life versus God when we came to this chapter. So, as we work through this chapter, we will be looking at this paradox that the good God allows evil to exist, and that bad things happen to good people.

Definition of Sovereignty

The best way I know of to define sovereignty is the right and ability to choose what and when to control. The monarchs of medieval Europe could not control every little thing that went on in their kingdoms. The same is true for the governments of today. It is necessary for the person or government in charge to decide exactly what is important enough to control, and what to let run on its own.

Governments are given this right and ability to choose by their people, either through fear, or free will. A dictator will obtain the right through fear and intimidation. A democratic leader will be given the right through a popular vote of the people. Once the decision is made, then the government has the right to control the situation, if not the ability.

God, as maker of the universe and all that is in it, has the right to rule over everything the universe contains. To some this seems like He is being a dictator because they do not want to give Him the control over their life. To others, He seems like a democratically elected official whom they love to have in charge. Either way, there is no one more qualified than God to run and control what He has created.

We have seen as we have worked through this study that God has the ability to do anything. If He chooses to control something, He has the resources within Himself to accomplish it. God never faces a situation where He comes up short of ability or resources to carry out His plan.

God chooses what and when to control. God, like the governments created by men, does not see the necessity in controlling every little detail of life. He knows every detail through His omniscience, and He is active through His omnipresence, but He chooses not to control. God decides what needs to be controlled, and when the appropriate time is for controlling it.

Laws God Has Designed

There are certain laws which God has designed to control the universe. These are areas where God has chosen to set up parameters so that He does not have to keep constant control over these areas. But, there are times when God does interfere with some of these laws. This is His right as the ruler. While the President of the United States is not above the law, God is. He does not often interfere with these laws, but when He does, He makes whatever point He is trying to get across.

The Laws of Nature

When God set up the natural universe He created laws to govern it. Scientists have found and use some of these laws. For instance, the laws of planetary motion have helped scientists locate planets in our solar system, even though we cannot see them. There are laws which govern our weather, which still confuses us, but scientists are getting better at predicting what will happen in tomorrow's weather. And, there are laws which govern the spread and cure of disease, which scientists are constantly discovering and applying. Each of these areas contains set laws in which God rarely intrudes upon. But, there are times when he proves that He is in control.

God has designed, and set into law, that the earth will rotate on its axis as it goes around the sun. Each rotation is to take twenty four hours. This rotation causes the light of the sun to move from east to west across the earth in a smooth movement. Early on people discovered this and made sun dials which could help them know what time of day it is. There are at least two times where the Bible mentions that this steady rotation of the earth was interrupted.

The first mention of an interruption in the rotation of the earth is found in the book of Joshua. Joshua was the man who took over the leadership of Israel after the death of Moses. He led the people on the military campaign to reclaim the land of Canaan, modern day Israel. During one of the campaigns Joshua and the Israeli army had the Amorites, one of the major tribes in the area, on the run. Joshua wanted to finish the job that day. He did not want night to fall and lose the enemy. So, he called out to God to stop the sun so they would continue to have daylight in which to fight (Joshua 10:12-14). The Bible says that God stopped the sun from moving for about a day. In other words, God miraculously intervened and stopped the rotation of the earth for about a day, or slowed it enough to lengthen the day. There is some speculation as to whether this event was local or global. Either way, God chose to suspend the law of planetary motion for that particular period of time, and at least in that particular area.

Joshua had the sun stop for about a day. Apparently it was not a full day. In the book of 2 Kings we find another account of the earth and sun not acting according to the natural laws. King Hezekiah, a very good king of Judah, lay sick and dying. He had been told by the prophet Isaiah that he should get his affairs in order because he was about to die. Hezekiah prayed to God. God decided to heal Hezekiah of his sickness. As a sign to confirm that he was not to die, Hezekiah asked for a sign. He wanted the shadow to move backwards on the sun-dial he could see from his window. God made the shadow move backward ten degrees (2 Kings 20:8-11). Once again, this could have been a localized event, but God still suspended the laws of planetary movement in that place and for that time by putting them in reverse. Most Bible scholars agree that this second movement for Hezekiah completed the full day of time left uncompleted by Joshua.

The weather is another area where there are set laws. High pressure gives clear skies, while low pressure brings the chance of rain and sometimes storms. When conditions are right, hurricanes are produced. Tornadoes and hail need specific atmospheric conditions in order to be manifested, and it needs to be around the freezing mark in order for snow to be produced.

Weather seems to be the one thing that God is not too afraid to mess with in the Bible. It is something that is localized and does not carry any real global ramifications. Well, sometimes it has global ramifications. Like that little thing Noah was involved in called the flood (Genesis 7-8). Talk about a change in the weather. God apparently cut loose with everything above ground and under ground.

There was a king of Israel named Ahab. He was a very wicked and evil king who had no intention of worshipping God. This caused God to tell the prophet Elijah that there would be no rain in Israel until He said so (1 Kings 17:1). There was a long drought in the land of Israel. Ahab became angry and started looking for water, and the head of Elijah. Finally God had Elijah set up a contest between him and the priests of the false god Baal. God won the contest and, after the false priests were killed, He told Elijah that rain was coming. Sure enough, a deluge of rain came (1 Kings 18:41-45). God changed the weather pattern around Israel to keep rain away, and then to bring rain when He wanted.

Jesus also displayed sovereignty over the weather. In Mark 4:35-41, Jesus and His disciples took a trip across the Sea of Galilee. This area is known for its sudden and violent storms. As they are crossing the water, one of these storms hits them and begins filling the boat with water. It must have been serious because experienced fishermen were scared of losing the ship. Jesus gets up and tells the storm to be still. Everything goes silent and the sea calms. The disciples are in awe of this person who can command the weather.

A little later in the book of Mark we see a similar situation. Only this time, Jesus sends His disciples in a boat ahead of Him. The storm arises and they are caught in it. Jesus takes a stroll on the water to reach their boat. As soon as He gets into the boat, the storm ceases (Mark 6:45-51). Jesus obviously had control over the weather, when He chose to have that control. Otherwise, He let it follow the laws set up for it by God.

Disease is part of the natural order of things, and is generally ruled by laws. Certain conditions seem to keep disease from starting or spreading, while other conditions promote its spread. But God has demonstrated that He can control disease when He wants. King David had disobeyed God by counting the people of Israel so he would know the size of the army he could muster. His dependence was on his army instead of on God for protection. God took exception to this and launched a plague into Israel, which decreased the population greatly (2 Samuel 24:15-16). But, when God decided He had given out enough punishment, He stopped the plague from spreading any further.

If you will simply scan the first four books of the New Testament you will find that Jesus constantly displayed sovereignty over disease. Jesus chose who would be healed. Not everyone around Him was instantly healed of all of their sickness. God is discriminating, even when it comes to healing people. But, that is His right. To heal everyone of everything all of the time would keep us from facing some of the consequences to our actions. This would not be right, and God knows that. However, there are times when God will intervene and override the laws set up to govern sickness and disease.

The Laws of Consequences

As we saw when we discussed justice and mercy, sin always causes negative consequences. Each and every action we take has a positive or a negative consequence. These consequences can either effect the person who did the action, or someone else, or both. God does not always choose to intervene in the consequences of our actions.

Genesis 3 shows us that God allowed Adam and Eve to suffer the consequences of their disobedience to God. But in the New Testament we see the culmination of God's overall plan to eliminate some of the consequences through the death of Jesus (Romans 5:18,19).

Joseph, one of the sons of Israel, was sold by his brothers into slavery and wound up in Egypt. This caused great sorrow for his father, and some hardship on his brothers. But God used this event to bring about good consequences. The land of Egypt was saved from starvation as God warned Joseph of a coming famine. That famine drove Joseph's family into Egypt so they would not starve. Joseph came to this conclusion about the consequences of his brother's actions: My brothers meant to do me harm, but God meant for good to happen to us (Genesis 50:20).

God could keep us from suffering bad consequences if He wanted. But that would not be good for us. Negative consequences help to keep us from doing what is wrong. Having a child sit in time out for an act of disobedience is a negative consequence, but it teaches them that what they did was wrong. Grounding a teenager for not making curfew is a negative consequence (which almost kills the teen), but it is necessary to get them to obey the rules you have laid down. God does not often choose to negate negative consequences because it would be detrimental to us if He did. God chooses the appropriate time and circumstance to intervene when it comes to consequences.

The Law of Love

When we discussed God being love, and wanting us to love Him, we fond out that true love cannot be forced into a person. In other words I cannot be made to love someone, and they cannot be made to love me. Love is a choice. That is the rule that God has no intention of ever changing, or adjusting, or even interfering with.

True love is hard to explain and define. It is the emotion which comes from the heart that makes a person want to put another person's needs and wants above his own. While it may feel like we are compelled to do this, because of the rush of emotion we sometimes feel for the other person, it is really a choice we make.

Romantic love with its rush of adrenaline and gushy feeling is not true love. It can come from true love, but it is not the total of love. Real love is deeper and more settled. Real love is when you see a person in need and decide to help him. The marriage based on real love is the one that lasts a lifetime instead of when it stops being fun. The choice to do what is best for someone else, even at your expense, is real love.

God will do things to get us to love Him. He has given us life, and He has died for us. But He will always let it be our choice to love Him. God does not want us to be robots that are programmed to say nice things about Him and do everything He wants. That really gives no gratification. It feels good to be loved by someone else because you know that they have chosen you. It would feel empty and hollow if you knew they were just pretending, or they had to act that way toward you.

God gets a kick out of loving us and being loved by us. He has wired us so that we enjoy loving and being loved. But it has to be our choice for who we love. God will never mess with that, because then it would not be real love.

The Law of Free Choice

This law is closely related to the law of love. God does not, and will not, hinder our ability to freely choose what direction we want to go, or what action we want to take. This is the one that is really hard to understand because each choice brings a consequence, sometimes negative. God could easily keep us from making wrong decisions and suffering negative consequences, but then we would be robots, just like if He were to force us to love.

We look around and we wonder why bad things happen. It is because God gave us free choice. All of us suffer the consequences of someone else's bad choices, and the consequences of our own bad choices. Negative consequences started with Adam and Eve's wrong decision to listen to someone other than God. We are still paying the price for that decision. All the evil in the world, all the disease, and even the natural disasters we face, all stem from that one wrong decision. It is perpetuated through the centuries by every person who walks the earth. When we say that life happens, we mean that we are feeling the effects of the good and bad choices all of us have made.

God knew when He created humans what the outcome would be. He knew the good and bad consequences of giving us free will. But, in the end, He decided it was worth it. Some people choose to reject God, and want Him to leave them alone. Others embrace God and love Him. In the end, God will give each person exactly what they chose in life. Some will spend eternity in a place where He does not make His presence known, others will live with him forever.

It is interesting to me that God never breaks this law of free choice. Search the Bible all you want, but you will never find an instance in which God forced someone to make a particular decision. The closest we get is when the Bible tells us that God hardened the heart of Pharaoh to not let the people of Israel leave Egypt (Exodus 7-11). But, this decision had already been made by Pharaoh. God just forced Him to hold to his decision in order to see the consequences of his attitude toward God and His people.

God never breaks the law of free choice or the law of love. To do so would destroy the relationship God desires to have with us. The relationship depends on both parties being able to honestly interact with the other. This is impossible where the will is not completely free.

Summary

God is completely sovereign. He rules everything. He truly has the right and ability to choose what and when to control. There are certain laws that He has put in place in order to keep things running in an orderly fashion. Sometimes He chooses to interfere with these laws, but He does not do so often or they would become exceptions instead of laws. There are some laws that God chooses to absolutely not mess with. He will not touch the laws of love and free choice. He will not jeopardize our relationship with Him.

Brush Strokes

God wants to be the ruler of our life, but, as we have just seen, that is our decision. Never would God insist on being the ruler of our life and making decisions for us. Instead, God communicates to us through His word to let us know what He is like, and to show us what are good and bad choices we could make. God encourages us to enter into a real relationship with Him instead of forcing us into being His puppets on a string.

So, maybe you are sitting there thinking that, from what you have read so far in this book, God is someone you could trust to have a relationship with. Maybe you are thinking that God does have your best interest at heart, and that He is the kind of person you would like to have in charge of your life. How do you enter into a relationship with God?

Believe it or not, God has made it simple for us. He has already done the hard work. Romans 6:23 tells us that the payment sin gives us is death. We have already seen that this is true when we looked at God being just. It was determined that sin was listening to someone other than God for our definition of right and wrong. This could only lead to death physically and spiritually.

Let me pause here and really define what I mean by spiritual death. This is important because this is the death we are talking about in relation to sin, especially when it relates to Romans 6:23. Man is made up of a physical body (this outside flesh we can see and touch), and a spiritual body, or soul/spirit, which we cannot see. We are alive as long as these two parts are together. Physically we die when the soul/spirit separates from the body. The soul/spirit dies when it is separated from the presence of God.

Remember Adam and Eve? God told them that they would die when they ate the fruit (Genesis 2:17). Physically they did not die the day they ate the fruit, but spiritually they did. God had always been close to Adam and Eve. But, after they sinned by listening to the serpent instead of to God, they no longer had that relationship with God. His presence was not continually there as it had been before. The soul/spirit within them died.

Because of the sin of Adam and Eve, everyone born into this world enters with a soul/spirit that is dead (Romans 5:12). Now a dead soul/spirit does not mean it is inanimate. A dead body has no animation to it, it does not move, and it eventually ceases to exist as it decomposes. But a spirit never stops existing, and is always animated. Its life and death depends on where it is in relationship with God. A soul/spirit that has a relationship with God is like a person who is free to roam around in the fresh air and sunshine. But, a soul/spirit that is separated from God is like a person who is confined in a dark and foul dungeon. That is what it means to be spiritually dead.

Every single person in this world has sinned, they have listened to someone other than God for a definition of right and wrong (Romans 3:10,23). Because of this, justice demands that we die physically, and spiritually.

But God loved us enough to pay the price justice demands so that He could give us mercy (Romans 5:8). Jesus lived the perfect life without sin, always getting His definition of right and wrong from God, and then He gave up His life. He paid the price justice demanded of us even though it was not demanded of Him. Because of that sacrifice Jesus made for us with His life, God can extend to us the offer of eternal spiritual life with him (Romans 6:23 the last part).

This offer is extended to us, but it is not forced on us. Remember, God will never interfere with our free choice. So, we must make the choice. Here are our options. We can either choose to spend our life and eternity without God (be spiritually dead), or we can choose to spend our life and eternity with God (be spiritually alive).

The first choice will have you spending eternity in a place where God does not make His presence known. This is known as hell. It is a terrible place to visit, and an even worse place to live for eternity. There is nothing good in hell. God is the source of everything that is good. Without His presence there can be nothing good there. Hell is described as a place of eternal fire and torment. Imagine extreme heat burning you, and total darkness around you. You can hear the screams coming from your own mouth, but you do not know if there is anyone there to hear you. Your worst nightmares plague you constantly. There is never any relief, never any let up in the pain and suffering.

God does not want anyone to have to suffer through hell (2 Peter 3:9). He wants us to choose the second option; the one that is with Him, the source of everything that is good, for eternity. Our relationship with him does not start at the time we die physically, it begins the moment we make the decision to have a relationship with God. While in this life, we will have a more peaceful attitude toward life. There are still many problems and challenges, but God is there to guide us through them. When our life here is over, then we will go to heaven. Imagine the most beautiful place you have ever seen, and you still won't get close to heaven's beauty. It is a place where there is only good because we only listen to God for our definition of right and wrong. We only do what is right, so there are no more negative consequences. There is never any let up in the joy and happiness we experience.

I'm hoping that no one chooses the first option. But, if you do, I cannot stop you, and neither will God. For those who want to choose the second option and enter into a relationship with God, what do you have to do? It is very simple. Romans 10:9,10 and 13, tell us that we must first believe that Jesus has paid the price demanded by justice for us. That is what it means by believing Jesus was raised from the dead. He was dead because of us, and He was raised because He did not deserve to die. In other words, we have to acknowledge the fact that we sin, and that Jesus paid the price for us.

Then, we simply ask God to be a part of our life. The passage in Romans uses the term Lord to refer to Jesus. Remember that Lord is the word used to denote sovereignty. What these verses are telling us is that we are to make God, Jesus, the Lord of our life. We are to allow Him to call the shots. This does not mean that if we mess up and sin again that the relationship with God is off and we have to start all over again. It does mean that we work hard at allowing God to control us instead of controlling ourselves.

To put all of this simply, read John 3:16. God saw the price we were going to have to pay for our sin. So He came and paid the price Himself. If we will just accept the fact that we need Him and ask Him into our life, God will give us eternal life. It is a gift, paid for by Him, we do not have to do anything to earn it.

If you want to enter into a relationship with God, then you can pray something like this: "Dear God, I know I have sinned and deserve the punishment of eternal separation from you. But, right now, I accept the payment Jesus made for me by dying to pay my debt for sin. Please enter my life, and be the Lord of my life. I want to have a relationship with you. Thank you."

God will always be true to honoring the decision you have made. He knows your heart. If you want Him in your life, He will be there. If you made that decision and prayed that prayer, then you now have a relationship with God. In order to grow in your relationship it is important that you find a local church to attend. Ask a coworker or friend what church they would recommend. A local church will provide you with the support you need as you grow in God and allow Him to rule in your life.

God Is Unchangeable

Change is something most of us resist, but all have to accept. It is what makes our life interesting. If everything were the same day after day, it would be so boring there would be no point in living. So, why is it so good that God does not change? What does it mean that God is unchangeable?

That is what we are going to look at as God puts His finishing touch on His portrait. If I am not mistaken, artists used to cover their paintings with some sort of lacquer or some substance in order to preserve the water colors or oils used. That is what God has done by showing us this characteristic. God is unchangeable. The fancy word for this is immutable, and it means constant, consistent, unchanging.

God's characteristics do not change.

The physical and moral characteristics of God never change. James 1:17 describes God as being light without any shadow to denote movement or change within Him. This verse speaks more to God's moral characteristics as James is trying to show that good things come from God because of His good moral nature. This means that the moral attributes of holiness, justice, love, mercy and truth will never change. They will always remain good. Never for a moment could God become evil. That would change His moral character, and He would cease being God.

The writer of Hebrews was focusing on the physical characteristics of God as He quotes from Psalm 102:25-27 (Hebrews 1:10-12). As solid as they are and as permanent as they may seem, the earth and universe will one day be destroyed. The writer of the Psalm describes it as God taking off His coat and putting on a new one. He contrasts this with the never changing and eternal nature of God. God will never stop being a spirit, or change form into something other than spirit. That is His essential nature. God will always be self-existent. He will remain a trinity and possess the qualities of omnipotence, omniscience and omnipresence.

These verses show us that while God does not change in His physical or moral being, He is still active and involved, constantly working. So, while God's being does not change, He is constantly working to enact change around Him. God is not a rock that sits there and cannot change anything around Him. He is active and powerful and creative.

When we get right down to it, God's own characteristics will not allow for change, and do not need change. 2 Timothy 2:13 tells us that God cannot deny who He is. In other words, God is perfect in all of His characteristics, including truth. For God to say that He needs to change something about Himself would be to say that He is not perfect. This would be untrue. His physical and moral perfections are absolute, and nothing needs to be changed because nothing can be made better. And, because God is perfectly holy and true, He cannot change for the worse. God is perfect in every way and does not need to change, and will not change. As the saying goes, why mess with perfection?

Jesus also does not change (Hebrews 13:8). Obviously the physical form of Jesus has changed. He had a body here on earth that was different than the body He had after the resurrection (He was able to enter a locked room John 20:19-20). But, as God, Jesus is spirit, and that did not change. All of His physical and moral characteristics He possesses as God have not and will not change.

God's laws and rules do not change.

Many people, when they are teenagers, feel that their parents are inconsistent with the rules that are laid down. This is especially true when there is more than one child in the house. Either the younger or the older feels that the other is getting special treatment.

Maybe you feel that way in the job you are in. The company wants something done one way this minute, and another way the next. The rules seem to change daily. If your work has anything to do with the law, you know that the law does seem to change daily as new court cases are heard and new laws passed. Governmental regulations are in a constant state of flux.

Thankfully, God is absolutely consistent and unchanging in His rules and laws (Psalm 33:11). What was wrong from the beginning is still wrong today, and will always be wrong. Those things God considers to be right will always be right. The Ten Commandments have not changed, and never will.

God's rules accomplish a twofold goal. The first is to keep us from suffering negative consequences. The second is to help support us and guide us in our relationship with God. These have always been God's objectives for us, and He has tailored His rules to see that they are accomplished. His objectives will never change, and so, the rules to achieve them will never change.

We will never wake up some day and hear God say, "Here is a new Bible, and a whole new set of rules to follow. I've decided to change the way I do business." God's rules, like His character, are perfect. They have been made to achieve His goals for us, and they do not need to change.

Now, someone may say, what about all of those sacrifices we read about in the Old Testament? Did God change the rules in the New Testament? The answer is no.

We have kind of touched on the sacrifices when we discussed the payment demanded by justice. The entire book of Hebrews addresses this very question. Let me see if I can give you a basic summary of the argument. The sacrifices of animals were made as a temporary solution to the payment for sin. These sacrifices always looked forward to the one perfect sacrifice that God would provide. The priests were continuously offering sacrifices for the people. But, when Jesus came and offered Himself as the sacrifice, those many sacrifices were no longer necessary. Jesus made one, perfect sacrifice to pay it all (Hebrews 10:11-13).

When it comes to the issues of the sacrifices, we all look to the perfect sacrifice. Those in the Old Testament had certain regulations to follow in their own sacrifices as they looked forward to the perfect sacrifice. We, in the New Testament era, look backward at the perfect sacrifice, completed for us. There was no change in God's law. Everyone is dealt with the same way. A sacrifice had to be made for the payment demanded by justice. It is just that some looked forward, while others look back.

God will never change the rules on us. His laws are steady, consistent and reliable.

God's promises must be kept.

We touched on the fact that God has to keep His promises when we talked about God being true. To not keep a promise is to change your mind, and to lie. God does neither. God's omniscience always allows Him to set in His mind what action is to be taken. He already knows what He will do before He says anything. He knows if He has the capacity to do it, and will not promise anything He cannot accomplish.

The writer of Hebrews says that when God made His promise to Abraham, He swore on His own character that He would accomplish what was promised (Hebrews 6:13-18). This oath was based on the fact that God could not lie and say He would do something when He had no intentions of doing it, or could not do it. And, it was based on the fact that God does not change. His truth would remain the same; therefore His promise must be fulfilled.

What was true of God with Abraham is true for us today. God must keep His promises.

God does not change the way He acts toward people's actions.

There are a couple of verses in the Bible that have given some people a little trouble when it comes to discussing God not changing His mind. The particular verses are Exodus 32:14, and Jonah 3:10. In these verses there is a word that the King James translates "repented." To repent means to change your mind about something and go a different, usually opposite, direction. There is no problem when the word repent is used in relation to people. But these verses have the word connected with God. This would be a problem if God actually changes His mind.

Let us look at the circumstances surrounding these two verses. After all, if we take a verse out of its context we run the risk of not getting the correct meaning. That is like taking a ten second sound bite out a politicians hour long speech and declaring that this is what he said. You have to put everything in context.

Moses received the Ten Commandments from God in Exodus 20. Moses came down from Mount Sinai and told the people what God had said. For further clarification, God told the people in Exodus 20:23 that they were not to make any gods of silver or gold. In chapter 24 God calls Moses back up to the mountain to give him more instructions about how the tabernacle (the worship center) was to be built.

Moses was on the mountain for a long time and the people got impatient. In Exodus 32 they made a calf of gold to represent their god. This made God very angry. The people were already disobeying Him. They were worshipping another god. God reacted by wanting to destroy all the people except for Moses (Exodus 32:7-10).

God's reaction was to the evil the people were doing in worshipping a false god. Moses though turned to God and pled for the people (Exodus 32:11-14). The goodness of Moses, and His attitude toward God saved the people. God did not change his mind about the actions of the people. He was still angry because they were wrong. But, he focused on the goodness of Moses and allowed Moses to have his request granted that the people live.

God had a choice to make. He could go ahead and destroy the people, which would hurt Moses, or allow the people to live and bless Moses. With this choice, God blessed Moses. But the people did not get off easy. If we read the rest of chapter 32, we find that Moses ground up their golden calf and made them drink it. He also called for those who were loyal to God to stand with Him. Then he gave the orders for these men to go and kill those who were against God. 3,000 people died. The final verse says that God plagued the people because of the golden calf they had made. God did not change His mind. There was still punishment for the people. But He chose to bless Moses and grant his request.

Maybe you have heard the story of Jonah and the whale (it was really a great fish). The book of Jonah in the Old Testament tells his story. Jonah was a prophet of God who did not like the people of Nineveh, the capital of Assyria, a country north of Israel. These people would eventually conquer Israel. God told Jonah to go to Nineveh and tell them that He was going to destroy the city because they were so evil.

Jonah decided to try to make a run for it and get away from this responsibility God had given him. He ends up on a ship headed the opposite direction. God sends a fierce storm, which scares the people Jonah is with. They throw him overboard and the storm stops. God sends a big fish to swallow Jonah and take him back to land. This was the first submarine ride.

Once back on land, Jonah goes to Nineveh and tells them that they are going to be destroyed. When the king gets the message, he tells everyone to go into mourning. They were not to eat any food, and were to turn from their evil ways (Jonah 3:5-9). The people repented. They changed the direction they were going. This is what God wanted in the first place.

God decided not to destroy Nineveh because the people had changed their attitude about the evil they were doing (Jonah 3:10). He was ready to punish their evil, but just as ready to forgive them and reward their goodness. God did not change the way He dealt with the people of Nineveh. He had always determined that He would punish their evil, but reward their good.

Numbers 23:19-21 tells us that God does not change His mind. The word in the King James translation is repent. This passage gives us a hint that our interpretation of the other two passages is correct. There is no contradiction. Balaam was a prophet for hire. He was hired by one of Israel's enemies to curse them. But, Balaam says that he cannot do that because God has not found anything wrong with Israel that they deserve to be cursed.

This shows us that God's actions toward people are determined by their actions toward Him, and toward evil. Israel had done nothing wrong to make

God deal with them differently. They did not deserve to be cursed. Had Israel been evil, then God would have cursed them, as we saw in the Exodus passage.

God's actions toward people are based on His reaction to right and wrong. He is going to reward good and punish evil. If someone changes their mind and decides to turn away from evil and do good, then God will stop planning punishment and start planning the reward. This is not a change of mind for God, it is being consistent with who He is.

Brush Strokes

For our final Brush Strokes we are going to look at the question of why God being unchangeable is good for us. Security is one of the basic needs in a person's life. The need to feel secure has to be met, or we miss out on developing emotionally.

God is completely secure. There can be no doubt that God will always be here with us. His presence will never leave. His power will never diminish, so He will keep providing for us. God will continue to know each of us intimately. The hairs on our head will continue to be numbered. His goodness will never subside, and His love will continue to do what is best for us. Is it any wonder that the Psalmist referred to God as his rock (Psalm 18:2,31,46)? Nothing and no one could be more secure.

We can be secure in the fact that God is going to be there to fulfill His promises to us. His ability to carry out those promises will still be there as well. If you made the decision to enter into a relationship with God in the last chapter, then you can be assured that God is going to be true to that relationship. He will never let you go. Your relationship with Him is eternal. And, when you leave this life, you will spend eternity with God in heaven. That is our great hope.

It is impossible to live life without hope. If we have no hope, then there is no purpose or reason for living. There is nothing to look forward to. No reason to get up in the morning and put your shoes on. Some people hope for things that will never happen. But our hope is in God. Since He never changes, our hope is as sure as if it has already happened. God gives us the ultimate hope of a continued life with Him. It is an unshakable hope because God, who promised, does not change.

So, God fulfills two needs in our life by being unchangeable. He gives us an unshakable sense of security. And, He provides an unfailing hope. To live life with those two things is beyond what most people experience. Do you want to have that experience?

Conclusion

I know that when you write a conclusion you are supposed to review all the important points in the book, or have some final words of wisdom to make people remember what they have read. But, when you view a painting, the most important thing is what it means to you. What is it that you feel when you look at the picture portrayed on the canvas? Unfortunately, I cannot speak for you. I cannot say what you felt, or learned, from gazing into this portrait God has given us of Himself. But, I can tell you what I have felt. So, if you will allow me, I would like to be very personal as we end this session of viewing.

From the very beginning I have never been as excited about a project as I have this one. From the moment I began planning it I could see possibilities, and had huge expectations. Fortunately, my expectations have been exceeded.

Writing the opening chapter blew me away. God didn't just crawl out of the box I had kept Him in for so many years; he leaped out and stomped it to dust. I began to get a deeper sense that God is way beyond my puny comprehension. That was not scary, it was exciting. God was a spirit being who could connect with my spirit. He communicated to me, through His words in the Bible, what He is like. I had barely scratched the surface. The first stroke of the Master's brush had left me desiring more.

It is hard to explain how the writing progressed, or how my awe of God grew. Some of the passages used to display the trinity were old to me, but took on a new light as I saw their meaning in relation to this truth. That would happen a lot in this study. The final words of Jesus to His disciples on the night He was betrayed opened up like never before. I saw the truth Jesus shared about the interaction of the trinity for the first time. It has been there all along, and I have read it before, but I had never seen it like this.

God's brush stroke displaying His self-existence and eternality was huge. It had never occurred to me that those two are inseparable. I saw that part of self-existence meant that God could donate life, and that is how He gives life to each of us, even me. And, when I realized that the scriptures were intentional in showing that Jesus had created life, I was humbled at how little I had previously known.

Working through the next three chapters made the box completely disappear. God is so much smarter and stronger than anything I could ever imagine. And yet, He is right here with me. He cares about me, and knows me better than I know myself. I am important to God.

The outline of the picture was taking shape. I had a new respect for God, and a better idea of what He is like. Now came the time to begin filling in the colors with His moral characteristics.

Before I started writing the chapter on holiness, I had a completely different view of it. I have always seen holiness in view of God's wrath, and that was scary. Holiness, to me, was the wall God kept around Himself to keep out things that were bad. But, that did not mesh with the portrait God was painting of Himself from the Bible. I cannot begin to describe to you how powerful a moment it was, and still is, to realize that the definition of holiness is "embracing what is right to the exclusion of what is wrong." For me this changed the color of holiness. It went from being a deep blood red of boiling anger, to an inviting, untarnished, golden yellow of utmost purity. Me, a sinner, an impure being, could be allowed close to God.

After looking long and hard at that part of the portrait, the other colors began to come more clearly into view. It took that change in my view of holiness to finally understand the part justice plays in the portrait of God. It really is the deep blood red of the portrait. Justice demanded death as the payment for my sin, and the sin of all others. That was only fair and just. It was a proper consequence to the action of sin.

The love of God is sometimes romanticized. Thankfully, I believe I have had a realistic look at the love of God that is both affectionate and corrective.

The fight between love and justice created the mercy of God. I have seen that part of the portrait so much that it was getting old to me. But this time, I saw it in a whole new light. The plan God conceived and the price He paid in order to be able to give me mercy. He paid justice out of love. Jesus paid with His own blood and death. I was struck with how unworthy I was of such a gift. But, then God reminded me that it is not mercy if it is deserved. Mercy is such an indescribably beautiful color.

God will keep His promises to me without fail. That was nothing new for me. But the promises are so much richer and deeper now than they were before.

I have been in awe the entire time I have been writing this. I have had a relationship with God for thirty four years and have been to Bible college. But, with each chapter, God showed me a new detail in His portrait I had missed previously. By the time I hit the last three characteristics I had no idea what to expect.

The chapter on wisdom I think surprised me the most. I did not see how I was going to be able to get a paragraph out of it. But when I began writing, things began to come to mind. I could see how this color blended with that color, how this line connected with another. Before I knew it, a chapter was done, and the wisdom of God had left me speechless.

God rules. And that is so true. This was another chapter I thought I would have trouble getting a paragraph written. Then, the definition of sovereignty came to me: "the right and ability to choose what and when to control." Once that definition entered my mind, the rest of the chapter came easily. The Brush Strokes in this chapter was the most important one. The whole point of God creating us and dying for us is to get us to have a relationship with Him. And, the best part of that relationship is letting God have control. If I follow God's ways, I'll be a lot happier and more peaceful in my life, no matter what the circumstances.

Sovereignty was the signature moment for the portrait. The portrait was complete as God had revealed all of Himself to us. He had shown us His true purpose in our living and His dying. The fact that God is unchangeable was the lacquer applied to preserve the painting so that it will never run, or smear, or fade.

This has been an awesome time for me. Looking at the portrait of God is so invigorating, humbling, exciting, and settling. I know that there will be times when I fail to look at the portrait of God. During those times I will forget some of what I have felt and learned here. The images in my mind will fade, but they can be renewed each time I return my gaze to His divine portrait. And when I return, I will once again see a line or a color I had never seen before.

If this experience has touched you half as much as it has touched me, then I am grateful that you have been able to experience it. Originally this project was to be shared with only a few people. But, early on in the writing I felt it needed to be shared with as many people as possible. If this book has touched you, then share it with your friends. It will give you something in common. And, perhaps, you will be able to get together and enter the gallery of the Bible yourselves in order to continue to view God's self portrait.

0-595-33463-6

Printed in the United States
23250LVS00006B/280-327